GRASS GAMES
&
MOON RACES

GRASS GAMES & MOON RACES

CALIFORNIA INDIAN GAMES AND TOYS

• • • •

Jeannine Gendar

HEYDAY BOOKS ◆ BERKELEY, CALIFORNIA

Publisher's Cataloging in Publication
   (Prepared by Quality Books, Inc.)
Gendar, Jeannine.
   Grass games and moon races: California Indian games and toys/ Jeannine Gendar.
   p. cm.
   Includes bibliographical references and index.
   ISBN 0-930588-56-8
   ISBN 978-0-930588-56-4

   1. Indians of North America--California--Games.   2. Indians of North America--California--Recreation.   I. Title.

E98.G2G46 1995   394'.3'09794
                                            QBI95-20282

Cover painting by L. Frank: "This is Yo Luck"

Published by:
Heyday Books
P.O. Box 9145
Berkeley, CA 94709
(510) 549-3564

Printed in the United States of America
10 9 8 7 6 5 4 3

For my mother

Acknowledgments

"The end is always better than the beginning." This old saying about basketry bemoans and celebrates the unevenness that comes from learning as we work, and it applies to writing as well. Now that the book is written, I feel I know which questions to ask. For their patience with me in getting to this point, and for their help, I thank Paul Apodaca, Pauline Bechtel, George Blake, Dot Brovarney, Parris Butler, Carey Caldwell, George French, Geoff Gamble, Joe Giovanetti, Leanne Hinton, Julian Lang, Sherrie Smith-Ferri, Tony Sylvia, and Jenny Watts. Acknowledgments are due several writers whose contributions to *News from Native California* were helpful with this book: Brian Bibby, Kathy Lewis, Bev Ortiz, Vicki Patterson, and David Peri, to name a few. And I cannot begin to describe the gratitude I feel toward the many others who have given me glimpses of what it means to be from California's native tribes.

My heartfelt thanks go to Malcolm Margolin, publisher of Heyday Books, for the inspiration, kindness, help, and fun he brought to the writing of this book, and to the delightful staff at Heyday: Amy Hunter, Wendy Low, Sadie Margolin, Yolanda Montijo, Ellen Trabilcy, and Robert Zermeño.

Special thanks go to the Windows on our World Foundation, which provided generous funds for the special issue of *News from Native California* that led to this book.

CONTENTS

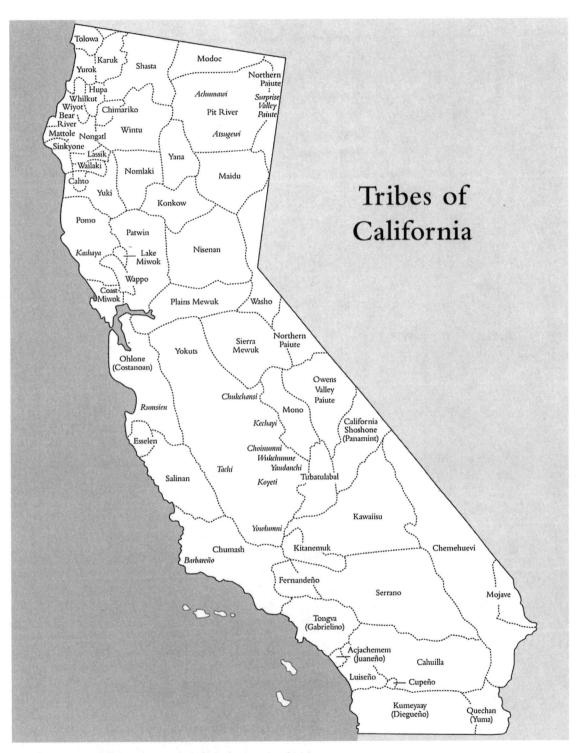

Tolowa
Karuk
Yurok
Shasta
Modoc
Hupa
Northern
Paiute
Whilkut
Achumawi
*Surprise
Valley
Paiute*
Wiyot
Chimariko
Pit River
Bear
River
Wintu
Atsugewi
Mattole
Nongatl
Sinkyone
Lassik
Yana
Wailaki
Nomlaki
Maidu
Cahto
Yuki
Konkow
Pomo
Patwin
Kashaya
Lake
Miwok
Nisenan
Wappo
Coast
Miwok
Plains Mewuk
Washo
Ohlone
(Costanoan)
Yokuts
Sierra
Mewuk
Northern
Paiute
Rumsien
Chukchansi
Owens
Valley
Paiute
Mono
Kechayi
California
Shoshone
(Panamint)
Esselen
Choinumni
Wukchumne
Yaudanchi
Tachi
Tubatulabal
Salinan
Koyeti
Kawaiisu
Yowlumni
Chumash
Kitanemuk
Chemehuevi
Barbareño
Fernandeño
Serrano
Mojave
Tongva
(Gabrielino)
Acjachemem
(Juaneño)
Cahuilla
Luiseño
Cupeño
Kumeyaay
(Diegueño)
Quechan
(Yuma)

Tribes of California

Subgroups are included on the map (in italics) when mentioned in the text.

GRASS GAMES
&
MOON RACES

INTRODUCTION

Grass games, in which players shuffle small pieces of deer bone wrapped with milkweed string; Indian footballs made of deerhide stuffed with soaproot fiber; bundles of sunflower leaves for archery targets; poles made of willow, hoops of yucca fiber, dolls of kelp; dice made from walnut shells filled with pine pitch: California's native games and toys are a reflection of the natural history of the state—its mountains, rivers, deserts, wetlands, woodlands, and seashore—and California's first people.

Tolowa, Shasta, Yurok, Karuk, Hupa, Wiyot, Modoc, Achumawi… these are the names of just a handful of California's tribes. At one time, there were as many as six hundred autonomous tribal groups in the state, with at least a hundred different languages and innumerable dialects. Today, nearly fifty of these languages are still spoken, although few non-Indian Californians are aware of this. Two hundred years of historic disasters, as California was overrun with missionaries, soldiers, miners, and other Euro-American immigrants, shattered the state's original cultures and it is only recently that native people have begun to pick up the pieces. This book is for them, in the hope that a compilation of information about games will be helpful, and for everyone else who is drawn to an older, and in some ways simpler, way of life.

Scholars love to speculate about the function of games: reenacting myth, imitating warfare, sublimating aggression, reinforcing social structures, and so on; and while this is certainly a fascinating area of research, it is not the focus of this book. I have included traditional stories and technical information, and I have tried, in all seriousness, to convey the place of games and toys in the heart of native cultures—but the ultimate purpose of this book is to promote fun.

With so many different tribes and so many different landscapes, it is no surprise that variations of California's native games abound; some are included here, some are not. Some of these games are still played, while others have faded away. Some descriptions can be based on experience or eyewitness accounts, but for others we must rely on sketchy ethnographic reports. For these reasons and because games evolve as they are played, readers should not consider the information in this book to be comprehensive or exhaustive. Those with more scholarly purposes and those who are trying to retrace the past of specific tribes will want to check the works listed in the bibliography.

Some games were played in winter, some in summer, some at night, some by day. In one tribe, women might play a game exclusively, while for their neighbors it might be a men's game. Pregnant or menstruating women might be considered unlucky or too powerful to be nearby. It might be considered very bad form to handle another person's gambling equipment. Some of these rules are included in this book, but the unfortunate fact is that this knowledge is not always available. Again, the bibliography may be helpful for more thorough research. The best way to learn these things, of course, is from people who have learned them from their own elders and ancestors. We can look forward to more of this as the rebirth of California cultures continues, as the memories of elders come to light, and as young people create memories of their own.

Karuk stick game players. Photo courtesy of Humboldt State University Special Collection, No. H-48.

Indian Football and Other Field Games

When they played *ama·ty* they caught the ball with small seedbeaters. They had a goal at each end. They started in the middle, and a man threw the ball up in the air for them by way of starting. A woman caught it by clapping the seedbeaters together. Then she threw it straight towards the goal. Another woman caught it and threw it back towards the other end and *their* goal.

They did this for a long time. Then a fast woman ran with it to their goal and threw it in. When they achieved this they won; they did this all day long. They sweated so they could not see. At night they fell into a death-like sleep, they were so tired. That was their game, that is what the women and girls did. That was their game in the early days.

William Joseph (Nisenan), 1930

Moving a ball toward a goal: what could be simpler? But as William Joseph's account indicates, simplicity doesn't diminish Native Californian passion for football-type games any more than it does the rest of the nation's. From the mountainous northwest to the southern deserts, people drove, tossed, or batted balls of mountain mahogany, braided buckskin, or polished stone, stuffed deerhide or seasoned laurel knots.

These games fall into two basic categories: those in which a team tries to move the ball or some other object toward its own goal and the other team tries to prevent it; and games in which both teams race to get the ball to a shared goal. Sometimes players kick the ball; sometimes they move it along or toss it with sticks; sometimes, as in the above account, they use racquets shaped like the baskets women traditionally used for gathering seeds. Local rules might allow players to pick the ball up and bat it, or hit it off a "tee," or maneuver it onto the tops of their feet and fling it—there were at least as many types of equipment and sets of rules as there were tribes playing the games. But sometimes all these variations caused trouble; contentious players of contemporary hockey might well have met their matches in early California:

> The Luiseños know how to play well, strong men. Once thirty Luiseños went off to San Juan [Mission San Juan Capistrano], another mission near the Mission of San Luis Rey de Francia, our mission. They arrived there and were invited to play ball. They said, "We want to, but let us make a rule that you cannot carry the ball in your hand." Those indeed said, "Thus we will do. We will play with all justice." Sunday during the afternoon the Luiseños [took] their sticks and [went] off to the place for the game.
>
> … All the people of this district were watching the game, and the captain of that district too was watching on horseback. All thirty Luiseños played well and were speedily defeating the Sanjuaneños, when one Sanjuaneño takes the ball and carries it in his hand. Then a Luiseño comes up, and seizing him by the waist throws him up and makes him fall. Another Sanjuaneño came to defend his countryman. Other Luiseños go to help the first. After these came the captain, and he beat a Luiseño. Then one of the Luiseños, stronger and with a huge body, gave a leap, knocked him down. The horse stepped on him and dragged him beneath his feet. He was not able to get up. Attracted by the uproar, the people came up with sticks in hand…

Pablo Tac (Luiseño), ca. 1835

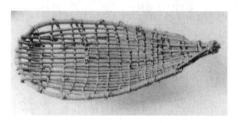

Top: A Maidu woman using a seedbeater to gather seeds. Photo courtesy of Field Museum, No. 1926. Below: A Mewuk racquet of the type used to play the amaty game described by William Joseph. Photo courtesy of Hearst Museum of Anthropology, No. 1-10356.

SHINNY

Not all versions of shinny—games in which the ball or puck is moved with a stick—are this rough. Cultural traditions, as well as natural factors like terrain and climate, might determine the intensity of play, the materials from which balls and sticks were made, the size of the field and the number of players on a team, the extent to which offense or defense was emphasized, and whether men, women, or both played the game in a given area or tribe. Almost universally, though, one goal won the game. This is surely an indication of the game's difficulty and the wholeheartedness with which it was played.

Nisenan women living in the foothills of California's Sierra Nevada, as well as Plains and Sierra Mewuk people living south of them, played the lacrosse-like game described at the beginning of this chapter, and they also had a shinny game, played with sticks and a heavy piece of rope (*tiki·li*) about 18 inches long:

> They threw it [the *tiki·li*] up in the air with that stick. Another woman caught it there with [her] stick. In that way they always threw towards their goal.…They did that for a long time. When a fast woman caught the *tiki·li* with her stick and ran with it, then when she got near the goal, she threw straight at the goal. Then another woman caught it and brought it back again towards their goal. When she did that all the women pursued her. When she had almost brought it there to the goal, the sticks clattered as they all tried to catch the *tiki·li*. One woman tossed it right through into the goal.
>
> Then they all tumbled over with fatigue. "Let us quit," they said. "We are tired," they said. "You win, let us leave it at that," they said.
>
> *William Joseph (Nisenan), 1930*

Stick Game

In 1916, Lucy Thompson described shinny, or "stick game" as it is often called in northwestern California, as played by her Yurok people and the nearby Hupa, Karuk, and Tolowa tribes:

> They select the giants, or the greatest athletes of the tribe, to make up the two teams.… Each side would put up large sums of money and valuable articles for their chosen team, which would cause much excitement in betting and gambling upon the games. The side of the victorious team would win large sums of Indian money, which would add to the wealth of their division and make them more powerful.…
>
> *Lucy Thompson (Yurok), 1916*

The northwestern California tribes still "play sticks," though usually just for special occasions. This is a very serious game, a reenactment of a game introduced to humans by the first inhabitants of the world. In the past, only adults played, after undergoing

Hupa tossles and stick, collected by Stewart Culin in 1900. The drawing is adapted from Culin's Games of the North American Indians. *The sticks on the tossle are 3 inches long, and the stick is 32 inches long.*

arduous training, but now elementary and high school students sometimes play for special school events.

The game is played on a field which may be small or large (as long as a football field), sandy or gravelly—it just depends on where the *ikxaréeyav,* or *woge,* or *kixunai,* as the first people are called by the Karuk, Yurok, and Hupa people respectively, ordained that a playing field should be. The players use sticks about three feet long, or the length of their legs, that are curved at one end. The ball, usually called a "tossle," is actually two round sticks three to five inches long tied together with a piece of buckskin. There are three players on a team.

Playing fields are oriented according to the Klamath River; "downriver" and "upriver" are directional terms that pervade every aspect of life in the Klamath/ Trinity area. As the game starts, players from the upriver and downriver teams pair off at points along the field. The pair in the middle has the tossle, and the other pairs stand with opponents facing each other, their sticks interlocked. One of the two players in the middle drops the tossle, and tries to catch the buckskin with his stick and throw the tossle toward the goal. Then he runs after it and tosses it again—if his opponent doesn't catch up with him, in which case they begin to wrestle. Meanwhile, the other players are engaged in wrestling matches that started as soon as the tossle first hit the ground. In Karuk tradition, it was Horsefly and Thunder who first played sticks, and when it thunders, it's because Thunder is throwing Horsefly down. The first side to disengage itself long enough to get the tossle to its goal (a line at the edge of the field) wins.

> The champion team is applauded and praised loudly by the immense crowds that gather to witness these interesting games. The players in their wild enthusiasm for the glorious laurels of victory usually clash together so roughly in their efforts to rescue the sticks [tossle] from the other players that occasionally some of their members get hurt, and often crippled for life....

As this quotation from Lucy Thompson indicates, this game is not for the faint of heart! It may be that in the coastal mountains of northwestern California, where one ridge follows right after another and large, flat spaces are hard to find, wrestling and grappling are more important in a game of this type than in the wide open spaces of the flatlands and deserts. Ultimately, though, generalizations are treacherous, whether they are based on landscape, gender, or some other factor. The traditional Tolowa game, played north of the Klamath and Trinity River tribes, reportedly involved some wrestling but not as much in the Yurok game; their version was a more open, running game. Slightly inland and south of the Klamath tribes, the Yuki minimized wrestling, but the game was still exhausting—it was common for players to collapse on the field, and cracked shins weren't rare. There was no grappling in the Wappo game. According to the anthropologist Robert Lowie, in the Washo women's game players "knocked one another down, fell on one another, and tripped up opponents with their sticks." The Wintu game was also a women's game and wrestling was a part of it. Perhaps Frank Latta's comment about shinny is the most telling:

> Among the Yokuts, shinny was a very rough game. We know this to be true of the game played by white boys, but we are assured that it was much rougher as played by the Indians. They would yell, push, and shove. There was such a perfect barrage of swinging clubs that anyone who got in the

A Yurok stick game at Johnsons, 1926. Photo courtesy of Humboldt State University Special Collections, No. RB-44.

SHINNY BALLS

There is a Mojave story in which Pukehane, with the help of Nume-peta, kills his younger brother by stealing his kneecap and some other bones. Not long after this, one of the slain man's wives gives birth. The baby, a boy, comes out singing. As he grows older, the boy watches Pukehane and Nume-peta playing shinny. Until his mother tells him, he doesn't know that the ball they are playing with is the kneecap they stole from his father. He turns himself into a lizard, and no one sees him grab the ball. After considering the other directions, he hits the ball into the west with a stick. It flies like a meteor, falls into the mountains and breaks them, killing the people who lived there. Pukehane and Nume-peta say, "That boy! I knew he would do it. He has killed all those people. He will kill us too." The boy can't hear them, but he knows what they are saying, and laughs and shouts as he runs on to other heroic adventures.

Apart from this notable exception, Mojave people made shinny balls from dried pumpkins and other squash, which were readily available because the Mojave and other desert tribes grew them in fertile mud left by the Colorado River. An example in *Games of the North American Indians* is about 4-1/2 inches in diameter.

Tribes in other regions also used materials that were readily acquired, often from an animal or plant that had other uses in their cultures. In the northwest, Hupa, Yurok, and Karuk people used sticks and buckskin to make tossles for playing sticks. To their southeast, the Yana used bones linked by string.

Further south, Pomo people used knots they found under the bark of exposed roots of California laurels (*Umbellularia californica*), hardening them by placing them in hot ashes for a week or two. As an alternative, they used the knee bones or the knobs from pelvic bones of elk.

In the Sierra foothills, people used soft materials such as rabbit skin, grass, soaproot fibers (*Chlorogalum*) or, in the eastern Sierra, the inner bark of sagebrush (*Artemisia tridentata*). Sometimes these soft materials were wrapped with string, probably from Indian hemp (*Apocynum* spp.) or milkweed (*Asclepias* spp.) before being stuffed into a piece of deerhide, gathered, and stitched.

Milkweed and Indian hemp were common in much of California, and some tribes simply used pieces of rope made from plant fibers, or braided strips of deerhide. These include the Surprise Valley Paiute, Nisenan, and Mono. (There was also a Mono ball made of mountain mahogany—*Cercocarpus betuloides*.) Nomlaki players used an eight-inch rope hoop.

In the San Joaquin Valley and south, some Yokuts games used hoops, others used hide stuffed with plant fibers, and some used balls of wood or polished stone. On the southern California coast, Chumash people played shinny with wooden balls. And besides dried squash, desert tribes sometimes used cordage, probably from Yucca (*Yucca* spp.)— the example in *Games of the North American Indians* is about 1-1/2 inches in diameter.

Pictured: Yokuts stone shinny balls, about 2-1/2 to 3 inches in diameter; a Sierra Mewuk ball, about 5 inches in diameter, made of deerhide stuffed with shredded soaproot fiber; and a Pomo shinny ball, about 4 inches in diameter, made from the knot on a laurel root.

way was certain to be hit on the shins. We are told by pioneers that in spite of all their roughness, it was entirely impersonal and they never saw a fight or a quarrel in connection with an Indian game.

Frank Latta, 1949

Shinny Variations

Generally, there were three to ten players on a shinny or stick game team. Rumsien Ohlone teams in the Monterey area, where the game was called by its Californio Spanish name, *pachon,* had twelve players each. Fields were anywhere from two hundred to two thousand feet long or more. Inland Pomo people played on fields ranging from a quarter to a half mile long. Their rules allowed for picking the ball up and batting it in the air as well as moving it along on the ground. According to anthropologist Edwin Loeb, it was not uncommon for players to faint from overexertion. Instead of a single shinny stick, Coastal Pomo players used hazel sticks attached to each other at the base by a net to drag the ball along. Loeb says the Clear Lake tribes thought the nets were highly unfair when the coastal tribes first came over the mountains with them.

Composition of teams. Besides the Nisenan, some of the other tribes who had a shinny game played exclusively by women were the Tolowa, Shasta, Atsugewi, Wintu, Washo, and Chukchansi Yokuts. The Tolowa, Sinkyone, Yana, Nomlaki, Surprise Valley Paiute, and Tubatulabal had games played only by men. Among the Cahto, men and women might play on the same team, or they might form teams of men against women. In Nomlaki, Mono, Owens Valley Paiute, and several Yokuts groups—Kechayi, Tachi, and Wukchumne—men and women might also play in the same game. If teams weren't arranged by gender, they might be composed of family, friends, co-villagers, or tribal members. In some tribes, teams formed according to moieties—social divisions not necessarily based on family, but aligned with, for instance, a particular animal or cardinal direction.

Object of the game. In most shinny and football games, teams tried to score by getting the ball past the other team and through goal posts, or into a hole, or by hitting a stake with it, but there are a few interesting variations. In the Tachi Yokuts game, each side has its own ball and its own goal post, and tries to be the first to hit the post.

BALL RACES

Maidu women, living north of Sacramento from the Sierra foothills to the Sacramento River, played with shinny sticks and a so-called double ball. Similar to the northwestern tossle, the double ball consisted of sticks or acorns tied together. Maidu

SHINNY STICKS

"…several highly prized shinny clubs were included in the equipment of every well-regulated [Yokuts] Indian household. Much labor was expended in preparing the club, and it was carefully cared for. Indians have told me that when they were children they hunted along the cut banks of streams for small saplings having a curved root exposed. The root and lower portion of the trunk were cut away and taken to the village. There they were carefully trimmed and whittled and scraped to shape and, while still green, seasoned and hardened in the fire. The result was a smooth, nicely balanced club, resembling the hockey club now used by white people."

Frank Latta, 1949

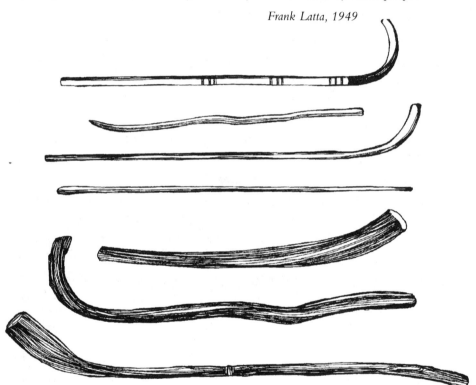

Pictured, from top: (1) Quechan shinny stick from Fort Yuma, 38-1/2 inches long. The outside of the curved end is painted black, the inner side red, and there are three sets of red and black painted bands on the stick; (2) Yurok shinny stick from the Klamath River area, hardwood, 33 inches long; (3) Mojave shinny stick, 41 inches long; (4) Shasta shinny stick from Hamburg Bar, peeled sapling about 40 inches long; (5) Kumeyaay shinny stick from Mesa Grande, 33 inches long; (6) Yokuts shinny stick from Tule River Reservation, 40 inches in length, made of oak, bent and fire-seasoned at the lower end, with a red stripe near the crook; (7) Mono shinny stick from Madera County, 54 inches long.

Drawings adapted from Games of the North American Indians.

players also used strips of hide braided together, or long bundles of bark. Sometimes they played shinny, moving the ball past opponents and toward opposite goals, but at other times the members of each team lined up, moving the ball from player to player in a race to get it to a single goal.

Maidu, Konkow, Nisenan, and Plains and Sierra Mewuk men and boys had a similar relay race, using a six to eight-inch ball made of buckskin stuffed with deer hair, soaproot fiber, moss, or shredded cedar bark. Instead of using sticks to move it, they kicked it.

Like shinny, this kind of ball race was played, with variations, throughout California. It must be an ancient game indeed, as it appears in many stories that took place in mythic times, when animals were people. The lively Yokuts story at the end of this chapter has the usual elements—a hero, with prowess, cunning, and help from relatives, has a ball race with a horrible villain.

The hero of the Owens Valley Paiute version, Tuhuki'ní' (Black Hawk), plays against Kiao'nu, who customarily beats, tortures, and cripples his opponents and then keeps them captive before eating them. With advice from his uncle, Crane, and help from his aunts, the Gophers, who make holes for Kiao'nu's ball to fall in, Tuhuki'ní' gets his ball around the course and past the goal first.

A similar Southern Sierra Mewuk story takes place in another world, the home of the birds that come from the south in the spring. In this version, Ku'tcu (a birdlike monster and the villain of the story), wins a race against Falcon's father and then kills him. Falcon later beats Ku'tcu by anticipating his tricks. A Central Sierra Mewuk version has Falcon winning a race against Mountain Sheep, with the help of Owl, Coyote, and Dove, who kick the ball along relay-style.

Atsugewi ball races

Humans reenacted these mythic events with an array of variations. In northeastern California, Atsugewi men (and probably other Pit River tribes) kicked the ball around a quarter-mile course, or sometimes around a lake.

Mono

Mono people, in the eastern part of the Kings River area and up into the Sierra Nevada, used sticks to hit the ball, starting at a goal hole, going around a post (without having to hit it), and returning to hit the ball into the hole. Four to six people played at a time—women sometimes played, but not in the same game with men. The length of the course varied with the number of players, but may have been at least seven miles long.

Yokuts

To the west, in the San Joaquin Valley and south to the Kern River area, Yokuts people had several variations. The Wukchumne version was much like the Mono game described above, except that players had to hit the turning post with their balls before heading back to the goal, and women did sometimes play opposite men. As is probably the case in the Mono game, this was a relay race with one player on a team hitting the ball along the course to the next. In the Wukchumne version, a player would hit the ball as many times as needed to get it to the next player in line, but in the Kechayi version the next player would come and get the ball. As soon as a team made a goal, they would take the ball out of the hole and start around the course again, and the first team to score a specified number of times won. Accounts vary and they are vague, but this number seems to have ranged from three to six, and there were from two to seven people on a team. Sometimes just two people would play, on a shortened course. To win this version, a player had to win six rounds in a row. The Wukchumne also played this game with hoops, and in another variation, played by the Wukchumne and other Yokuts groups, players hurled a ball made of polished stone or an oak burl wrapped tightly with buckskin—with their feet.

Cahuilla, Chumash, Quechan

In southern California, the Cahuilla played on two-man teams, kicking wooden balls that were reportedly somewhat smaller than croquet balls, for several miles and then back again. The Chumash version, called *gome* ("rubber") by the Spanish, used a ball about twice as big as a billiard ball. In the desert, two or more Quechan men would race, using mesquite balls about three inches in diameter. Each racer would lift the ball with his foot, fling it as far as possible, chase after it, and fling it again. The race took place along a course two to fives mile long, and then back again.

INDIAN FOOTBALL

The Nisenan and Sierra Mewuk people also had an "Indian football" game, as it is called, which is still popular today, especially at big times—special occasions when Indian people from all over California and others get together to celebrate and enjoy each others' company. The ball, about five or six inches in diameter, is made of rabbit fur or soft grass wrapped with string and covered with buckskin. The field is about a hundred yards long, with goal posts set about six feet apart at either end. Men and women play against each other in this game, in which each team tries to score by getting the ball through its own goal posts. Women are allowed to use their hands to throw the ball or pick it up and run with it, but men only use their feet. Some players act as goalies, keeping the ball from going through the posts, but as William Joseph's description tells us, the defense that takes place in the middle of the field can be even more important:

The men hugged the woman who carried the ball. When they tickled her belly, she threw the ball to another woman. If that woman missed, a man kicked the ball with the foot. Another woman caught it with the hands and ran with it towards their goal. Then a man hugged her again. When he threw her on the ground and rolled her around, she threw the ball. In that way another woman caught it and brought it towards their goal.... That was their playing together so that a man could hug the woman he loved. The women on their part took every opportunity to hug the men they loved. That game was like that so that this could be done.

William Joseph (Nisenan), 1930

Making a ball from materials at hand, or a shinny stick to season and cherish throughout the years; chasing the ball through open spaces for five miles or more, or lining up across vast meadows and gentle rises for a seven-mile relay race; men and women, children and adults competing fiercely and living together peacefully: to imagine this is to imagine the beauty of California's past. Surely this is reason enough to bring traditional games into the present.

Limik's Race

After Limik [Prairie Falcon] finished his fine *oo'-trutch* (flute) he played and played it all the time. There was one nice girl in his camp. He liked that girl. He said to himself, "Maybe I'm gonna marry that girl." So he went by her house and played and played and played. But she didn't pay any attention to him. She was just cooking and fixing acorn bread, and she didn't look at him. One day Limik asked that girl, "Why don't you talk to me? Why don't you look at me? I want to marry you. What's the matter with me?" That girl said, "I guess you're all right, but you chew *saw'-kawn* [Indian tobacco] all the time and you're dirty. Your mouth stinks."

Limik had one sister. He told that sister, "You get me one hair from the top of that girl's head. I want one hair from her head." So Limik's sister goes and talks and talks to that girl. Limik hangs one *pih-sa'-sin* [string covered with eagle down] on the tree by his house and he sits under that tree and plays and plays.

Limik's sister tells that girl, "You come here and sit down. I'll comb your hair." That girl don't think anything. She comes and sits down.

Pretty soon Limik's sister is combing that girl's hair. She combs and combs and combs. Then, quick, she pulls one hair out of the top of that girl's head. That girl jumps and gets mad. She says, "What are you taking my hair for? Give me my hair. I think maybe you are *he-ow'-trah* [mean] and you're gonna do something to me."

Limik's sister put that hair between two fingers. She held up her hands, front then back. That girl couldn't see that hair.

Pretty soon, Limik's sister came home. Limik asked, "Did you get that hair?" His sister said, "Yes, I got it. She got mad, but I got it anyway. Here it is."

Limik put that hair in his *oo'-trutch* flute. Next morning he got up early. Then he began playing and playing. That girl heard that playing. Maybe Limik was *trip'-nee* [had special powers] now. Anyway, that girl heard him. She got up and started to his house. She couldn't help it. She wanted to go. When she got there she saw Limik starting out to visit that gambler, Coo'-choon. She kept following him. He went about a half mile. Then he stopped. That girl caught up to him. Limik asked her, "Where are you going? Why are you following me?"

That girl said she wanted to go with Limik. Limik said, "No, I am going a long way. You go back home. You might get tired, you might get hungry if you follow me." That girl said, "Well, I want to go anyway." Finally Limik said, "All right, you can go, but don't you come near me. You stay away from me. I chew *saw'-kawn* and my mouth stinks."

Then they went on. Limik went ahead, and that girl was following, following behind all the time. Three nights that girl wanted to marry Limik, but every time, he said, "No. I chew *saw'-kawn*, my mouth stinks."

Pretty soon they came to Coo'-choon's house. Limik had an aunt living there. Coo'-choon didn't see Limik coming. Coo'-choon was away off at the north, at Choom'-nah pahn'-in, where the ground ends and where the world stops off in a big bluff. He was playing shinny with some people up there. He was on his way home when Limik got to his place. Limik's aunt told Limik not to let Coo'-choon see that girl following him or he'd kill her. So the aunt hid that girl.

Coo'-choon had killed lots of people playing Indian shinny. He won them, then he killed them. Lots of widows were there—Coo'-choon won their husbands playing shinny. Some people just lost a nose, maybe an eye, maybe an ear. Coyote lost his tail. Ground Owl lost one leg. Lots of them old people lost something playing shinny with Coo'-choon.

When Coo'-choon got close to his house, he saw Limik. He had heard about Limik lots of times. He knew Limik right away. He said, "Hello, *He-ow-trah* [mean fellow], I'm going to play you shinny. I'm going to burn you up."

Coo'-choon saw that nice woman who had been following Limik. He said, "You've got a wife? Maybe I'll win her." Limik said, "No, she's not my wife. She's just following me. She wants to marry me. But she can't marry me, my mouth stinks."

That Coo'-choon, he wanted to play that night. But Limik, he said, "No, just as well wait till morning." That night Limik played his *oo'-trutch*. He played and played. That gave him good luck to play the next day. Coo'-choon saw that. He didn't like it. He went into his house and danced with his *chah'-pit* [basketry gambling tray].

Next morning they're gonna start. Coo'-choon says, "Here, I've got a good stick. You want to use it?" Limik looks at that stick. It looks all right but he thinks, "Maybe it's all crooked inside." So he decides to use his own stick. Coo'-choon says, "Here, take my ball. I've got a good one." Limik looks at that ball. It's all painted red. Maybe it's *trip'-nee*. But Limik puts his hand on his kneecap. He says, "This is my ball. I'd better use it." Then he takes his ball out of his knee. Coo'-choon sees that and he thinks, "That's bad. Maybe this fellow, he's *trip'-nee*." But he can't help it, Limik can use his own ball.

Then, just before they are going to start, Coo'-choon calls to all the people. They all come around close to look. Some have no eyes, some have no nose, no leg, no hand, no tail. Coo-choon won them all playing shinny. Coo'-choon says, "Better you build a big fire. Just as soon as I win this game, I'm gonna burn this fellow, *He-ow'-trah*. Make a good big fire. We'll be through pretty soon."

Just before they started that game, Limik's aunt came out of her house and sat beside where they were going to bring that ball back [the goal]. That place where they would put that ball when they came back was a hole in an oak tree, way up high. That oak tree was hollow and the hole went way down in the ground to another *pahn* [world]. Coo'-choon didn't know that was Limik's aunt. Before they started, Limik took one *pih-sa'-sin* [eagle down string] and hung it on a limb by his aunt. He told his aunt, "If that stays there I'm going to win. If it falls down you know I'm gonna lose."

They got the *aw'-luls* [balls] ready and then they started. Right away Coo'-choon ran way ahead. He hit his ball and ran and ran away to the west. Pretty soon Limik thought, "I've got to do something pretty quick or that fellow is going to win me sure." Then he chewed some *saw'-kawn*. He asked the fog to come in. The fog came and Coo'-choon lost his *aw'-lul*. He ran around and around and when he found his ball and got out of that fog, Limik was way ahead. Coo'-choon yelled at Limik, "That's all right, *He-ow'-trah*, I'm gonna win you anyway." Pretty quick Coo'-choon was way ahead again.

Then Limik got out his *poo-lee chee-nah* [strong Indian tobacco]. He chewed some of it. Then they got to a lot of big oak trees that had those red and black *aw-paw'-pish* balls on them. Coo'-choon hit his ball. It hit one of those oak trees and all the *aw-paw'-pish* fell on the ground. Coo'-choon couldn't tell his ball from all the rest of them. He ran around and around and hit all of them. They all went crooked. It was a long time before he found his *aw'-lul*. Then he ran as fast as he could. When he passed

Limik, he made a bad wind so Limik couldn't run so fast. He always did that when he passed Limik.

Limik ate some more of that *poo-lee chee-nah*. When they came to a bog, Coo'-choon's ball sank down in the mud. He hit and hit and hit and had to dig his ball out of the mud. He yelled at Limik, "That's all right, *He-ow'-trah*, I'm gonna catch you anyway. I'm gonna win you and burn you up. Then, no more *He-ow'-trah.*" When he passed Limik again he made another bad wind and made Limik sick. Soon, Coo'-choon was way ahead again.

Limik chewed some more of that *poo-lee chee-nah*. Then he said, "I wish there was big water here. Then maybe that Coo'-choon would drown." That water came, but maybe Coo'-choon was *trip'-nee* too, because he didn't drown. He splashed and splashed and hit and hit. Then he got out of that water and he went on. He said, "I don't care, *He-ow'-trah*, I'm gonna catch you anyway."

Then, at the same time, they both got to that place where they were gonna hit their balls at that hole high up in that oak tree. Coo'-choon said, "You go ahead." Limik said, "No, this is your country, you go first."

So Coo'-choon got ready and hit his ball hard and straight. Limik's aunt was sitting by that tree. She had *trip'-nee chah'-pit*. She threw that *chah'-pit* up and it went over that hole. Coo'-choon's *aw'-lul* hit that *chah'-pit* and fell on the ground.

Then Limik hit his *aw'-lul*. His aunt drew in her breath quick, and made a noise like sucking. That Limik's ball went right in that hole and he won.

All those people, they laughed and laughed. Coyote hollered and hollered. He jumped 'round and 'round. All those people were gonna get their eyes, ears, noses, maybe legs back again.

—adapted from a story told by Henry Lawrence (Yowlumni) to Frank Latta in 1939

Drawing of a Mojave hoop and pole game, courtesy of the Bancroft Library, University of California.

As Happy as it is Possible for Human Beings to Be

Hoop and Pole Games

Each rancheria had a gaming court at, or near, its center. This court is made by smoothing the earth and tamping it solid. It was then covered with fine sand, and many games were played upon it. Here was always an excited, shouting, yelling, laughing group, generally intent upon their game and as carefree and happy as it is possible for human beings to be.

"The game I remember best was played with a hoop and a pole about ten feet long. The pole was about the same size as one of their fish spears. The hoop was made of bark coiled into a flat disc and held together with slender willow shoots. The disc was about one and one half feet in diameter and had a hole in the center about two or three inches in diameter.

"Any and everyone played this game. Sides were chosen and one person selected from each side to roll the disc. These two persons stood about twenty or thirty yards apart and at each end of the game court. They rolled the disc back and forth between them. The game was to throw a pole through the disc as it rolled by. For each pole thrown through the disc, two points were awarded to the side having the lucky or accurate player. If the pole passed only partly through and knocked the disc over, it counted only one point.

"The players lined up on each side of the course where the disc was rolled. They laughed and yelled and made a great deal of noise at this game and did all they could to rattle the opposing players when they were about to throw a pole. This was a great deal more exciting than you might think just from reading about it. When the disc was rolled across the court as many as thirty or forty poles would go flying through the air and the biggest problem in the game was to dodge the poles that came from the other side. They kept the score by calling it aloud much as we keep score in a game of horseshoes."

Thomas Jefferson Mayfield, 1928

This is an excerpt from *Indian Summer*, the remarkable memoirs of Thomas Jefferson Mayfield, a miner's son who lived with the Choinumni Yokuts people in California's San Joaquin Valley for much of his childhood, in the 1850s and 1860s. The hoop and pole game that Mayfield describes was immensely popular throughout much of North

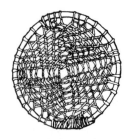

A netted hoop like those used by Cheyenne players and many others, but few California tribes.

America. Except for the northwestern part of the state, it was played in all of California, but it was among the Colorado River tribes—the Mojave, Chemehuevi, and Quechan—that passion for this game reached its peak. People usually gambled at dice and guessing games in California, but in the desert, the big stakes were on hoop and pole games.

According to Stewart Culin in *Games of the North American Indians*, this game was played exclusively by men.* Culin concludes that the netted hoop used by many tribes (but few in California) represents the net shield of the twin war gods who appear in many Native American cultures. I haven't come across anyone, historic or contemporary, who could corroborate this with reference to California tribes, but it is entirely likely that the California tribes who played this game did so within their own mythic contexts. According to the Mojave origin story, one of the first things Mastamho, the originator of Mojave culture, did was create a playing court. Then he brought the people there and told them that some would be foot racers, some would sing, some would dance, and some would gamble at the hoop and pole game. The game appears frequently in the saga of ancient Mojave history—it must have been one of the people's main pastimes—and in myth it is an explanation for all kinds of cosmic phenomena. In a hoop and pole contest Sun, after losing to the hero Ahta-hane, climbs to the top of his pole. Ahta-hane figures that Sun is going to try to get out of paying his debt by dropping fire on him, so he creates ice to put out the fire. This is when Sun escapes to the sky and becomes the sun that we know.

The favored game of the Mohave was between two players, each of whom cast a long pole at a rolling hoop. The ring was thrown by the

*This differs from some accounts, including Mayfield's statement that "any and everyone played" the Choinumni Yokuts game, but for the sake of simplicity I have only used male pronouns in this chapter.

winner of the last point, and either runner was at liberty to dart his pole when he pleased. If the hoop was pierced, nothing was counted. If the ring rested on the pole with sufficient overlap that a space was visible, one point was made. Should the ring lie on the end of the pole, the score was double. If both players cast successfully, both scored. Four points won the stakes. A favorite device was to hurl one's pole between the opponent's and the hoop.

A.L. Kroeber, 1925

This is an entirely different game from the Choinumni version described by Thomas Jefferson Mayfield. The poles are probably longer than the Choinumni poles, and the disk is a simple bark hoop wrapped with yucca fiber, about seven inches in diameter, while the Choinumni disk is a foot and a half in diameter, but with an opening of only three inches. As we look at versions played in other parts of the state, we'll see that there are plenty of other variables. There might be only one hoop, or each player might have one of his own. The poles might be thrown at the hoop from behind, in front, or at right angles. Sometimes players threw arrows instead of poles, and sometimes they shot the arrows. Sometimes they didn't actually throw the pole, but tried to catch the hoop on the pole without letting go of it. Sometimes they tried to send the pole all the way through the hoop, and sometimes they tried to stop the hoop so that it rested on the pole. In the Mojave version, you got a better score if you stopped the hoop just at the end of the pole. All of these possibilities were scored in different ways, and of course the number of points that made up a game varied from one tribe to another. Sometimes players stood still as they threw their poles, and sometimes they chased after the hoop. In some versions a player rolled the hoop for himself, but in others a teammate or an opponent might roll it. The number of players varied, as well as the number of people who were throwing poles or shooting arrows at any given moment. Here are some variations from around California. (Most of this information is based on old written accounts, and the details are sometimes sketchy.)

Northeast: Atsugewi and Surprise Valley Paiute

Instead of throwing poles, the Atsugewi people of northeastern California shot arrows at a rolling hoop. Surprise Valley Paiutes, also in the northeast, threw arrows instead of shooting them. They also sometimes used seven-foot, sharpened poles of green willow. In this game, a team of about five players would line up, and they would all, at the same time, try to throw their poles at a six-inch rolling hoop so that it landed on the pole. If no one succeeded, the hoop was rolled once more. If anyone succeeded, each of the others on his team would, in turn, move to the spot from which the successful player had thrown and try to hit the hoop where it had landed,

Two Yuma (probably Quechan) men ready to play hoop and pole. Photo courtesy of the Huntington Library, San Marino, California (Pierce 02555, no date).

Yuma (probably Quechan) men playing hoop and pole. Photo courtesy of the Huntington Library, San Marino, California (Pierce 02581, no date).

forfeiting a pole if he missed. Each player started with two poles, and the last team that had poles to throw with won.

Eastern Sierra: Owens Valley Paiute

Further south, on the eastern side of the Sierra Nevada, the Owens Valley Paiutes played in two-man teams, on a fifty-foot court with a foul line across the center. A member of each team would stand on each half of the court. A player on one side would roll the hoop, and then he and the opponent on his half of the court would throw their willow poles at it. Touching the hoop with the pole counted one point, and piercing it counted two. On the other half of the court, the partner of the player who had just made the best throw (come closest to the hoop) would get to roll the hoop; as in all games, defense was important, and there were tricks to rolling the hoop for one's own benefit.

North Central California: Pomo and Wappo

Near what is now Ukiah, Northern Pomo players used a 16-inch wooden hoop wrapped with dogbane (Indian hemp, *Apocynum)* and 9-foot poles. In this version, four players stand in corners of a 60-foot square court, and a back-up player stands near each one. Player One rolls the hoop rapidly toward Player Two, who uses his pole to try to catch the hoop as it passes him, but without letting the pole leave his hands, or he's out of the game. If he misses the hoop, his back-up player steps in and rolls the hoop to Player Three. Play continues, with the hoop going to Player Four and then to the first corner again. The last player left wins the stakes.

The Eastern Pomo hoop, about a foot in diameter, was made by bending split oak while it was still green, and hardening it in hot ashes. Two concentric strips would then be lashed together, with joints opposite each other. Poles were four or five feet long. Men would line up on opposite sides of a fifty-foot playing area. A player from one side would roll the hoop as hard as he could at the other side. As in the Northern Pomo game, a player on this side would try to catch the hoop on his pole, without letting go of the pole or letting it touch the ground. This counted as one point. The first side kept rolling the hoop until someone on the other side missed, and then the other side would roll. Twelve points made a game. Nearby, the Wappo people played essentially the same game, except that the hoop was made of hazel and measured two or three feet in diameter, the pole was about ten feet long, and there were six points to a game.

Monterey Bay Area: Rumsien Ohlone

Jean François de La Pérouse described the Rumsien Ohlone game as he observed it in the Monterey Bay area in the late 18th century:

They have two games to which they dedicate their whole leisure. The first, to which they give the name of *takersia*, consists in throwing and rolling a small hoop of three inches in diameter, in a space of ten square toises [one toise is 6.395 feet], cleared of grass and surrounded with fascines [bundles of sticks to enclose the court]. Each of the two players holds a stick of the size of a common cane, and five feet long; they endeavor to pass this stick into the hoop whilst it is in motion; if they succeed in this they gain two points; and if the hoop, when it stops, simply rests upon their stick, they gain one by it; the game is three points. This game is a violent exercise because the hoop or stick is always in action.

Linda Yamane, a Rumsien Ohlone descendent, described her efforts to play the game in 1994, based on La Pérouse and other written accounts. "At first I just couldn't believe the hoop could have been three inches in diameter. I wondered how it would be heavy enough or stable enough to roll across the ground for any useful length of time. But when I made the rings of strips of inner bark, they rolled along with ease. What isn't so easy, however, is trying to throw a five-foot pole through a rolling three-inch ring."

Sierra Foothills: Nisenan and Sierra Mewuk

The Nisenan hoop was made of two concentric rings: a 24-inch outer ring of oak wrapped with rawhide, and an inner rawhide hoop attached to the outer one with ten rawhide spokes. Players would roll the hoop, quickly move to a position at right angles to its path, and throw their nine-foot poles at it. Piercing the inner hoop counted ten points, hitting between the spokes five, and a "lean-up" two.

Mewuk players used a hoop of California lilac *(Ceanothus* spp.) or western chokecherry *(Prunus virginiana)* about one foot in diameter and wrapped with buckskin, and willow poles about five feet long. Some accounts describe hoops thirty inches in diameter made from oak, and poles as long as ten feet. Each player had several poles. One of the players would roll the hoop, and his opponent would throw a pole at it as it approached edge-on. If the thrower succeeded in putting the pole through the hoop, he would get one of the opponent's poles and another try. They played until one player had all the poles. Here is Dr. John Hudson's description of another Mewuk version of hoop and pole, this one resembling the Surprise Valley Paiute game:

A Sierra Mewuk hoop and pole made by Lucy Parker in 1994. The hoop is about a foot in diameter and made of wood wrapped with buckskin, and the pole, about five feet long, is willow.

The game is played by four players, who face each other on opposite sides of a square ninety feet across.

The casters, each of whom has four lances, stand opposite to each other, while two assistants, one for each side, roll the hoop across. As the wheel rolls, both casters throw at it, each trying to transfix it. If one is successful his opponent comes across to his place, and standing in the successful caster's tracks, tries to transfix the fallen hoop. After him, the first player tries at the same mark and from the same position. They cast alternately until all have thrown their four lances. The greater number of transfixing spears decides. There are 30 counting sticks, 15 to a side.

—in *Stewart Culin's* Games of the North American Indians

San Joaquin Valley: Yokuts

In the Choinumni Yokuts game described by Thomas Jefferson Mayfield at the beginning of this chapter, as many as thirty players at a time might be throwing poles at the rolling hoop. Mayfield describes another Choinumni game played only by men:

A small perforated stone was rolled instead of the disc. This stone was about three or four inches in diameter and had a hole in the center about an inch in diameter. This game was played principally by the young men. It was a much quieter game than the disc game, but was scored in the same way. They shot wooden pointed arrows at the stone as it passed by. This same stone was used to straighten their arrows and their shafts for gigging fish.

Nearby, Wukchumne Yokuts players aimed not to pierce the hoop but to cause it to fall on top of the pole as it came to rest. In a Chukchansi Yokuts version, the players rolled the hoops, about 3-1/2 inches in diameter, for themselves: one player would roll the hoop and then try to throw his pole through it for five points. If the hoop fell on the pole, he scored three points. If he failed the next player tried, and so on. The Koyeti Yokuts version was similar, with an added twist—if a thrower succeeded in striking the rolling hoop, he not only scored six points, but won the opportunity to put his hand over the other player's eyes on his next throw! The total score for a game was ten points.

Coastal Southern California: Chumash, Tongva, Fernandeño

In southern California, Barbareño Chumash people shot arrows at barrel-shaped stone disks about four inches long and three inches in diameter, the object being to pierce the disk while it was still in motion. Tongva (Gabrielino) and Fernandeño players used reed poles and four-inch hoops of willow wrapped with buckskin, trying to stop their hoops so that they laid on the pole, three points to a game. This game, and that of the Luiseños, may have been played by two partners at a time: first one team would throw, and they would get a certain number of points if either or both of their poles landed on the ring or pierced it. Then the opposing team would play, and so forth.

Southernmost California: Kumeyaay

In *Southern Diegueño Customs*, Leslie Spier describes a Kumeyaay game. The players used a hoop about six inches in diameter, made of mescal fibers and wrapped with more of the same to a thickness of about three quarters of an inch, and poles about ten feet long with either one or two grooves cut into the butt end. They didn't play on a court, but would set a distant point, sometimes a mile or more away, to play toward. Spier says the hoop "was held vertically, palm up, against the wrist, and thrown forward and down to roll." After a short run, the players would throw their poles, trying to bring the hoop to rest in one of the grooves cut into the pole or extending off either end of it. Stopping the hoop in a groove counted three points; extending it off the front end of the pole counted one point; off the throwing end counted three points. If the hoop stopped somewhere in the middle of the pole or if the pole went entirely through the hoop, no points were scored. The player who won the point threw the hoop the next time, and six points won the game. According to players Spier interviewed, "The hoop is a woman of whom one dreams. If she likes the player he will win no matter how the pole may be thrown. But if she is jealous, because the man sleeps with another, she will give the game to his opponent."

Except for a few solitary efforts to reconstitute it from ethnographic accounts, native people are not playing this game anymore in California. It surprised me to learn this—by all accounts it is a lively game, and has that combination of simplicity and infinite potential for improvement that makes a game truly engaging, even addictive. Some of the details of play are missing from the accounts that this chapter is based on, and this is why I included so much information about the variations from one tribe to the next; there are so many ways to play this game that a person trying to revive it, even without a conclusive description of any one version, could probably put together something that is true to what was played in the past, in spirit if not in every detail. This raises an interesting question: How hard and fast were the rules of these games? Did they change under the influence of travelers from other tribes? When someone thought up something new? Or maybe players on any given day might pick and choose from the possibilities, much as contemporary players choose a game of rummy or hearts or bridge from the same deck of cards.

Bow, arrows and quiver by Hupa/Yurok artist George Blake, ca. 1990. Photo by Rudy Gillard.

Bows and Arrows,
Sticks and Stones

There's a wonderful scene in Charles McNichols' novel about Mojave country, *Crazy Weather,* in which two boys who have been doing some hard traveling are feeling irritable. After a while, Havek kicks a small, round gourd out ahead of them and shoots an arrow at it. South Boy can't resist—he shoots, his arrow splits the gourd, "and pride lift[s] his heart." They carry on, each competing with himself and the other to make the best shot. In no time, they have forgotten their troubles. We should all be so fortunate—to be, like Havek and South Boy, so engrossed in what we are learning that we practice it every chance we get. And we should all be blessed with a life in which survival and entertainment, work and play, are sometimes integrated.

BOWS AND ARROWS

The type of bow most native Californians made was about three to four feet long, carved from a curved branch, backed with sinew for strength, and strung against the natural curve of the wood—a powerful form. Some southern California tribes used bows of this type, but the southern bows were often self-bowing—curved in the same direction, whether strung or not—and longer. Mojave bows were from four and a half to six feet long.

Bow materials ranged from yew, hazel, elder, and ash to mesquite, willow, and palm-leaf stem. Sinew was used for string, as were Indian hemp and milkweed fibers. According to George Foster in *Summary of Yuki Culture,* "A powerful man and bow reputedly could send an arrow for a quarter of a mile," and distance-shooting competitions were actually contests of strength.

California Indian archers often made two-piece arrows: a main shaft with a foreshaft set it into it. A hardwood foreshaft stabilized the flight of main shafts made of reed or

A Pomo man in armor, with bow and war arrows. Photo courtesy of the Field Museum, No. 11803.

other hollow materials, and if the point was damaged or stuck, another foreshaft could be used in the same arrow, saving some of the painstaking labor of making a new one. Cane *(Phragmites* spp.), being rigid and hollow, was favored for main shafts, along with syringa *(Philadelphus lewissii,* also called mock orange or arrowwood) and arrowweed *(Pluchea sericia).*

Obsidian was, and is, the favored material for points. As Lonnie Bill, a modern-day Mono arrowmaker says, "What makes this rock good is that it comes up from the center of the earth. She spit it out, and it's a tool for us… This is her gift to us, besides everything else."

One-piece arrows with sharpened ends, blunt wooden points, or no point at all were used for hunting small game at close range, and war arrows were often one piece with no point—the danger was not so much in being shot through the skin, but in failing to recover from the impact of a massive number of blunt missiles.

For practice, depending on the local ecology, people might shoot at targets made of sunflower leaves (Atsugewi), tule (Yuki), bundles of arrowweed (Quechan), grass (Nomlaki), or maybe a hat. Boys might shoot at bark "ducks" or throw spears at them. Sometimes a player would shoot an arrow into the ground, and then everyone would shoot to see who could get closest to it. Or a man might throw a bundle of grass with his bow hand and try to hit it before it reached the ground. People shot arrows through hoops suspended from branches, at marks on trees, through arches stuck in the ground, or at buried targets.

Then, when we want to practice shooting at a target, we go and gather canes. We make many canes into arrows. We make arrows well. We put feathers on them. Then, having finished the arrows, we make the target. We tie the brush. We practice shooting at that. Then whoever hits it hides the target under the ground. Then one of the boys says "shoot," and you shoot at the target now hidden underground. The one who hid the target shoots next. He hits that target, because he knows his own hiding place. He pulls out that target with his own arrow shot into it. Then he hides the target for another player. "Now shoot," he says, and the other player shoots. Then the one who hid the target shoots. He hits that target. Then they pay him one arrow. Some go back to their own houses without arrows, when they lose.

adapted from recollections of Yukaya, also called Mike Miranda
(Tubatulabal), 1934

Almost universally, people gambled for arrows in shooting games. In a Quechan game, players would throw a bundle about three inches in diameter made of arrowweed tips as far away as possible, then take turns shooting at it. A player would receive one

arrow from each of the other players if he hit the target, and the game would continue until one player had all the arrows. He would then throw the bundle into the air and shoot at it with the arrows he had won from the others. If he hit the bundle he kept the arrow, and if he missed he gave it back.

In *Southern Diegueño Customs,* Leslie Spier describes a game in which "two parties shoot at each other with arrows lacking foreshafts." Judging from the frequent appearance of dodging in stories, this Kumeyaay game was not unique to that tribe. Here is part of a Mewuk story from mythic times, when all the animals were talking about their own special skills:

California Jay said, "I do not think that you can hit me. You can try and try. Thus I will sing, when I dodge your arrows. Thus I will do, when I tire you. I do not believe that you can hit me. I eat nothing but acorns. That is what makes me so lively… Are you a good dodger? Are you a good dodger? You are going to fight me with the

A studio photograph of Quechan men. Note the long bow and blunt-tipped arrows. Photo courtesy of National Museum of the American Indian, No. 36020.

arrow," he said to Brown Wren. "I shall dodge you while I am seated. I shall dodge you while I am seated. I do not think that you can hit me after I have arranged my hair. You can try. You can try, but you will find that I am a good dodger."

Thomas Williams (Central Sierra Mewuk), ca. 1913

And here is another dodger, from Chemehuevi myth:

When Southern Fox left his home in Wiyaatuw[a], the Whipple Range, to visit his northern cousin, Blue Jay, he travelled in the following manner: stringing his bow from end to end with arrows, he discharged them all at once, outran them in their flight, and being like Coyote, a good dodger, he dodged them as they fell to earth around him. Then he collected the arrows. Whenever he pulled out one that had pierced the earth, water sprang forth.

Carobeth Laird, 1976

In an Owens Valley Paiute game, a player shoots arrows with cross-sticks on their points over his opponent, who tries to catch them in a basket, or a netted, rawhide hoop about a foot in diameter. And a Surprise Valley Paiute game is played much the same way, except that instead of trying to catch arrows in a basket, a player tries to position a hoop so that arrows thrown by an opponent go through it. He returns the arrows he misses, and keeps the ones he catches. This game is played for seven or eight points.

THROWING GAMES

There is also a Washo game in which you throw arrows instead of shooting them. A player stands sixty feet away from a target arrow that is stuck in the ground so that it leans in his direction, and throws a blunt, three-foot arrow at it. The next player steps up to the same place and tries to hit the leaning arrow or knock the other player's arrow out of the way, and so on. Any number of people can play. Hitting the target arrow or knocking another one away counts for one point, and dislodging the target arrow counts five.

Games in which players throw objects at a goal and try to knock each others' pieces away from it are common. A Kumeyaay game, for instance, is played much the same way as the Washo game, but with sandstone disks instead of arrows. In the Wukchumne Yokuts chip and pole game, players try to shove a small piece of wood toward a stake by throwing a pole at it, using a long, underhand motion. The chip is made of peeled willow, about two inches wide by four inches long. If one player's chip is near the stake, another tries to block it with his own. Moving an opponent's chip along with your own gains extra points.

In a similar game, often called snow-snake, players use an underhand throw to slide poles along the ground (sometimes in the snow), trying to get them to go farther than those of their fellow players. This game was played throughout North America. In California it was played by Pomo, Nisenan, Mewuk, and Wintu people, and probably others. Poles ranged from four to eight feet long, and were sometimes decorated to indicate ownership. The Nisenan pole was somewhat flattened on one end and pointed on the other. The Wintu version involved sliding four-foot saplings toward a stone or a stake.

In a Pomo "skating arrow" game played by boys, special arrows are thrown toward a low mound so that they glance off it and keep traveling. The arrows are about three feet long and three quarters of an inch in diameter, made of red willow or boxwood, and decorated by charring designs into the bark and then peeling the bark away. Players throw the arrows from the shoulder, using an index finger to propel them:

> The boy whose arrow traveled the farthest won; the boy whose arrow traveled the shortest distance got a crack on the "crazy bone" of his elbow from each of the other players. If he lost twice, he got two blows from each, and so on until he stopped playing. It was considered a sign of weakness to stop for this reason. Consequently the players often came in with their arms numb and swollen from this treatment.
>
> *Edwin Loeb, 1926*

Nomlaki, Eastern Pomo, Mewuk, and probably other tribes also had target practice with spears, often at bundles of tule or grass. In a Nisenan game, players threw their spears, chased after them, picked them up and threw them again, racing for a distant goal line.

In a Chukchansi Yokuts game, players would put up a ten to fifteen-foot screen of branches and place a post on each side, about ten feet away from the screen. Then, with one team on each side of the screen, they would throw long sticks, trying to hit the post concealed on the other side of the screen. An umpire stood at the end of the court where he could see the results, and the side with a stick nearest its post won a point.

When the rules and implements of the game are simple, there is always an opportunity for sport and something to bet. During root-digging season, Atsugewi men would bet roots on who could come closest to throwing a double-ended digging stick so that it stood straight up and down where it stuck in the earth.

The Making of Arrows

What shall we do, brother? What shall we do? I would like to hunt. I do not know how we are to hunt. I do not know how we are to hunt. I do not know how we shall be able to hunt. I should like very much to hunt. I do not know how we can make arrows. We have nothing with which to cut. We know of nothing with which to cut. I do not know how we can hunt. We have nothing with which to cut. We do not know how to cut. I would like very much to hunt, brother. I do not know how we are to arrange it, but we will try. We have nothing with which to cut. I should like you and me to hunt together, brother. We have nothing with which to hunt."

"Let us throw our grandmother into the water. If she does not want to go, we will pull her in. We will throw the old woman, our grandmother, into the water. After you have thrown her into the water, pull her out quickly. Pull her out quickly. Do not keep her in the water long. Do not keep her in the water long."

Then Dove went. Dove went. He threw his grandmother into the water, threw her into the water. After he had thrown her into the water, he pulled her out quickly. He pulled her out quickly.

Then Dove went to his brother and said, "I threw her into the water. I have already thrown her into the water. Come, I have her."

His brother said to him, "Pull one of her teeth. We will make a knife of it." Then he pulled one of her teeth, pulled one of her teeth. After they obtained the tooth, they commenced to cut, commenced to cut.

Then Prairie Falcon said, "Pull sinew from her arm. Pull sinew from her leg. We shall then have the cord for the bow." Thus spoke Prairie Falcon to his brother.

Dove obtained the sinew, as he was bid. Then they started to work on the arrows. They did not know how to begin. They made the arrows just by thinking. They made the bow. One of them told the other, "We will try." They made a good bow. They made a good bow. Nobody knew what the bow was. No one had ever seen a bow.

After they completed it, they looked at it. Prairie Falcon said to his brother, "I guess this will be satisfactory to hunt with." He told his brother to cut a piece of yellow pine. Thus spoke Prairie Falcon to his brother, after they had killed their grandmother. Then they cut the yellow pine with a knife made from their grandmother's tooth.

Their grandmother went into the water and cried and worried about herself. She said, "I did not think my boys would treat me this way."

The two brothers finished making their arrows and bows. They completed them. Prairie Falcon said, "These arrows are satisfactory. Let us try them." Thus spoke Prairie Falcon to Dove.

"We will see who can shoot the farthest." They shot toward the east end of the world. The arrows struck in the same place. The arrows struck in the same place. They did not strike in different places. They hit in the same place. After they had shot their arrows, Prairie Falcon said, "Let us race. Let us race. We will run to the place where the arrows struck. We will see who shot the farthest. We will see who shot the farthest."

Then they ran. Both started at the same time. Both started together. They both ran at the same speed. They ran together. One of them did not gain on the other. At last they reached the arrows. They arrived at the place where the arrows struck. Prairie Falcon said to Dove, "You are a pretty good runner. We both run about the same. Let us shoot again. Let us shoot again."

Then they shot toward the west end of the world. Again they ran to the place where the arrows struck. Neither won the race for they both ran together. Prairie Falcon said to Dove, "We run the same. We run the same. I did not think that you could run so fast."

They shot their arrows again toward the east. The arrows struck in one place. Then they ran. When they arrived at the arrows, both stopped at the same instant. They both stopped at the same time.

They shot again to the west end of the world. They shot toward the west. Then they ran to the place where the arrows struck. The arrows struck in a bush. When the brothers arrived, they saw the bush. One brother said to the other, "Let us dig this bush. It is good to eat. Let us dig it." They dug the bush from the lower side. Then they dug, dug, dug. They were nearing the end of the bush, nearing the end. They ate the bush as they dug. They ate while they dug. The root became thicker while they dug. They continued to dig, continued to dig. The younger brother said to the other, "Keep on digging. You will find the end pretty soon. Keep on digging." The older brother asked, "Do you see the end yet?" The younger one replied, "I am getting close to the end." He continued to dig. He continued to dig.

Then the grandmother, who had turned into Beaver, said, "I will have revenge upon those boys." She told the water to drown Prairie Falcon. The water came, while Prairie Falcon was digging, and drowned him. Dove escaped. He cried for his brother. He rolled and rolled over the hills. He cried for his dead brother. He rolled and rolled around the great mountains. He was scratched and bruised by the rocks and the brush. He bled all over. He mourned for his brother and cried for him. He said to himself, "I do not know what killed my brother." Thus he spoke to himself. He travelled all over the world crying, travelled to the place which he and his brother had visited together.

Dove met Spark. Spark asked him, "What are you doing? What are you crying about?" Dove replied, "Something killed my brother. I do not know what it was." Then Dove sent Spark to investigate. Spark alighted close to the old woman. The old woman was still crushing bones. She was still crushing bones. A small bone flew out of the mortar. Spark seized it and put it on an arrow. Then he shot the arrow with the bone point toward Dove. The arrow struck in front of Dove, while he was crying. Dove picked up the arrow and looked at the point. As he was about to remove the bone point, it spoke to him. The point turned into Prairie Falcon. After the bone arrow-point transformed itself into Prairie Falcon, Prairie Falcon cried for his brother Dove, because the latter had so many wounds and bruises.

Prairie Falcon cried and cried over his brother Dove, because the latter had bruised and hurt himself so. Brother Dove was bleeding. He had no hair. Then Prairie Falcon called the various kinds of birds together. He asked each to give him one feather. He said, "My brother has no feathers on him. Do me this favor. Give me one feather apiece." They each gave him one feather. Then he rehabilitated his brother Dove. He still cried for his brother Dove, for he felt sorry to think that Dove had cut and bruised himself so for him.

Then they went all over the world, searching for Dove's blood on the rocks, where he had struck. Every time that Prairie Falcon saw a rock with his brother's blood upon it he cried, for he knew that it was his brother's blood and that those were the rocks which had cut his brother.

Dove recovered from his bruises and cuts and was soon well again. Dove said to his brother, "I am well now. Worry about me no more. Worry about me no more. Do not trouble about me. I do not want to lose you. See how poor you look now." Thus spoke Dove to his brother, while he was crying. This made Prairie Falcon cry the more.

Dove continued, "I thought you told me the truth, when you said that that bush was good to eat. If I had known that you were to be taken away from me so suddenly, I should not have let you dig that bush. That is why I do not want you to bother with anything after this. Our grandmother turned into Beaver just as you fell, brother. If we had not attacked our grandmother, we should have had a grandmother still." Thus spoke Dove to his brother, Prairie Falcon.

Now they had no grandmother. Prairie Falcon cried because his grandmother had turned into Beaver. They both cried and cried for their grandmother. They did not know how to get back their grandmother. They went along the river. They saw Beaver in the riffle. They said, "There is Beaver." Beaver was their grandmother.

They used to take their grandmother everywhere they went, but they lost their grandmother because of the arrows. At last they abandoned the search for her and went home. Their grandmother had turned into Beaver.

Everybody made arrows thereafter. Dove cried for his grandmother. Prairie Falcon cried, but they made arrows. They lost their grandmother because of the arrows.

Thomas Williams (Central Sierra Mewuk), ca. 1913

A game of peon at the Pechanga Reservation (Luiseño) in the early 1960s. Left to right: Ed LaChapa, Leroy Salgado, and Billy Salgado. Photo by Ralph Michelsen, courtesy of the San Diego Museum of Man, No. 24245.

The Tensest of Wills,
the Keenest Perceptions

Hand Game

It's late September in the foothills of the Sierra Nevada. It's just the right time to pick up cones full of pine nuts, and the oaks are packed with acorns. The air is hot and the ground is dusty after the long California summer. In the shade of a ramada, a few people sit sipping diet sodas and iced tea after lunch. As the dishes are cleared away, a few more bring lawn chairs over. A low, quiet hum of anticipation starts up as people from tribes around the foothills and beyond greet each other, some of them taking their places in two long, opposing rows. Off to the side, someone is keeping track of bets, and spectators are finding comfortable spots. Now the kerchiefs and bones and counters come out, and the singing begins.

On the side that is singing, almost all the players are women, and the air is filled with sweet sound as their voices rise lightly to the lilting song, accompanied by the rhythmic clacking of split-stick clappers. Over and over and over again, they sing the same notes and syllables. Meanwhile, in time to the music, two players on their side are moving their hands around under kerchiefs that they hold out in front of themselves. Their faces are free of expression, except perhaps a slightly arrogant confidence. The kerchiefs are colorful, just the right weight to mask the players' graceful motions, fluttering slightly but not slipping around too much.

Under the kerchiefs, each player holds a pair of bones from the leg of a deer. The bones are about three inches long. One has a piece of string tied around its middle, and the other is plain. As the music continues, one player stops moving her hands around except to bob them tantalizingly up and down in place under the kerchief. Soon, the other player sits with arms crossed in front of her chest, fists tightly closed

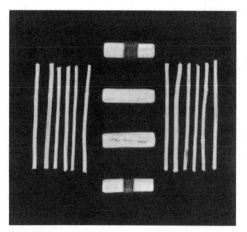

Pomo hand game bones and game counters. Photo by Scott Patterson courtesy of the Grace Hudson Museum.

and the kerchief dangling from one hand, face completely inscrutable.

The singing continues. A few flies spin around a pole, dust settles ever so slowly in the wake of children running by. A player on the other side lifts his arm and points, fingers arranged to show that he thinks each player has the unmarked bone in her outside hand. As the singing continues, the two players slowly and rhythmically open their hands to reveal… he was right.

This is "hand game," the classic Native American guessing game, played California-style. It is sometimes called grass game, because people used to hide the bones in bundles of dry grass, and in southern California and parts of the Southwest it is called peon (pronounced as in Spanish, with *e* sounding like *ay* in "hay" and *o* as in "own").

The guesser was right about both sets of bones, so they go over to his side. He handles them for a moment and then passes one set to his right, to a stately woman about fifty years old, and one pair to a very young woman on his left. She looks anxious for a split second, but then she composes her face and picks up a kerchief. Its colors are fresh and it looks a little stiff as the she moves her hands gracefully beneath it. There are more men on this side, the singing is lower and heavier. The volume builds as a young man on the other side, the name of his tribe emblazoned on his bright red t-shirt, makes the guess, indicating with a stylized gesture that both players hold the unmarked bone in their right hands. One player, the younger of the two, opens her hand to show that he is right. She passes the bones to the other side. But he was wrong about the other player, so his side gives up a counter stick, the singing continues, and the victor hides the bones again.

As the game continues, players find plenty of ways to disturb their opponents. A good-looking young man tries to embarrass an even younger woman. A singer rattles his clapper stick with subtle but unmistakable triumph at each bad guess. And everyone puts as much power into the singing as possible, to build up their confidence and daunt their opponents. Later in the game, the player with the new kerchief proves to be a skillful guesser. The young man in the t-shirt also makes a string of good guesses, but an old man on the other side finally fools him. All the players are graceful and determined, and no one is ever truly rude. In the background people watch for hours, talking quietly, keeping an eye on the kids, humming along beneath their breath, maybe making side bets. The sun goes down, the light of the full moon falls on the treetops, and the singing goes on and on.

"It is a game in which not sticks and luck but the tensest of wills, the keenest perceptions, and the supplest of muscular responses are matched," wrote Alfred Kroeber, around 1919. "There is possibly no game in the world that, played sitting, has, with equal intrinsic simplicity, such competitive capacities." Nineteenth and early twentieth century anthropologists and journalists wrote detailed and glowing accounts of hand game and peon. A paragraph from an 1888 edition of the *Escondido Times* illustrates their fascination with the game:

> We should like to be able to picture the intense interest the visitors took in the game, the wild antics of the players, the umpire stolid and watching every motion, the fire burning between the players, lighting up their faces and bringing out in bold relief every expression of disgust or pleasure, making up a picture long to be remembered. To anyone wishing to break himself of the fascinating game of poker, we should recommend Peone.

The young woman on the right is guessing how the women on the left have hidden the bones in this picture of Mono gambling. In the middle, an "umpire" holds the counters. Photo courtesy of Grace Hudson Museum (No. 15334).

A Washo hand game in 1995. Left to right: Benny Fillmore holding the bones under a piece of deerhide; Lyle Mills; John Snooks, Jr.; and John Snooks. To the left, outside the game, are Helen Fillmore and Amanda Mills. Photo by Laura Fillmore.

A good guesser doesn't restrict his or her observation to an opponent's hands, but takes the language of the entire body into account, not to mention past experience with the same player, a lifetime of developing intuition, and perhaps some specific charms or activities for cultivating power. And the player who hides the bones must be equally astute. One Yuki player told the ethnographer George Foster, "You can pretty nearly always judge where a player is going to guess." Some versions of the game include the possibility of making a false guess for the purpose of gleaning clues. A Tubatulabal guesser might point from side to side at the person holding the bones, meanwhile watching closely, then announce a real guess by clapping and then pointing. An Owens Valley Paiute player of the 1930s would make a number of guesses, and then before the real one exclaim, "Here!"

Of all the traditional California games, hand game is the one that best survived the devastating impact of Europeans on native California cultures. In 1937, Foster observed that Yuki women had just begun to take up hand game, which in Yuki tradition had been played only by men, "when it was finally abandoned." But not long after, Walter Goldschmidt reported, in his *Nomlaki Ethnography,* that "native games had seemingly given way to card games when in 1939 the use of bone gambling reappeared."

The game described at the beginning of this chapter took place in 1994. One of the players used a small, round drum instead of clapper sticks, and some of the songs included little bits of English. One of the players used an old-style deerhide "blanket," as they are called, to hide the bones, instead of a kerchief. For some tribes at least, hand game used to be for men only, but by the late 19th century women played on the same teams with men, or opposing teams, or in their own games. Peon is played only by men, though women participate by singing, and in northwestern California only men play "Indian cards."

Methods of Play

There are variations without number in the way hand game can be played, and one of its many virtues is that it is independent of language. The words and gestures for each possible guess are easily learned, and the words of the songs are almost always vocables—words without literal meaning. Played at intervillage and intertribal celebrations, constantly subject to new influences, hand game has always crossed cultural and geographic boundaries, but its essence remains intact.

These days, people usually play hand game with two sets of bones, so that two players on a team are hiding them at once. There are descriptions of Chumash, Ohlone, Tubatulabal, Wintu, Yana, and other games in which one player hides just one bone (or stick or stone or bead or shell), and the player on the other side guesses in which hand it is hidden. One person at a time does the guessing, though there was at least one Yokuts version in which, if a large number of people were playing at once, two people guessed (nothing would be revealed until both guesses were made, and the guessing side would get a point for each correct guess, but both guesses would have to be correct for the side to get the bones).

Which side starts the game? In Yuki tradition, the challenger would hide the bones first. In the past, Sierra Mewuk players would decide with a "pregame," in which each team would have a pair of bones, and the other side would try to guess their locations, relinquishing a counter stick with each wrong guess, until they guessed right. Then

John Snooks and Gene Wilkinson playing hand game at the Washo reservation near Gardnerville, Nevada, 1995. Photo by Laura Fillmore.

GUESSING

Here are a few examples of the gestures used to guess where the bones are in hand game. (Pointing with the index finger is bad manners or worse in some cultures.) Whether people are guessing for the plain or the marked bones varies from one tribe to the next; this information and accompanying words are included where available. In some traditions, the plain bones are considered female, the marked ones male. In some traditions this is reversed, and in some there is no male/female designation, or at least none was ever recorded.

SURPRISE VALLEY PAIUTE (plain)	Hold out right hand, palm downward	*ka'su'kwan*
YUKI	Point toward center hands	*húyit*
NOMLAKI (marked)	Raise one finger	*winempom*
SIERRA MEWUK (plain)	Hold both hands out with palm open and thumb pointing upward	*lee-lek*
OWENS VALLEY PAIUTE	Hold palm horizontal	

SURPRISE VALLEY PAIUTE	Extend right hand, thumb up, and move it vertically, pointing between the hiders	*tasi'güwai*
YUKI	Raise two fingers on one or both hands	*háli* or *mililalmik*
NOMLAKI	Raise two fingers	*toi'*
SIERRA MEWUK	Hold right hand out with palm open and thumb pointing upward	
OWENS VALLEY PAIUTE	Hold palm vertical	

SURPRISE VALLEY PAIUTE	Wave to the right	*siki'ba*★
YUKI	Make a sweeping motion from unmarked to marked bones	*he* or *haíke*
NOMLAKI	Hold out right hand	*tep*
SIERRA MEWUK	Use left hand across front to point to unmarked bones	*tek-muh*
OWENS VALLEY PAIUTE	Point left	

SURPRISE VALLEY PAIUTE	Wave to the left	*siki'ba*★
YUKI	Make a sweeping motion from unmarked to marked bones	*he* or *níhini*
NOMLAKI	Hold out left hand	*tcalisen*
SIERRA MEWUK	Use right hand across front to point to unmarked bones	
OWENS VALLEY PAIUTE	Point right	

★Isabel Kelly tells us, in *Ethnography of the Surprise Valley Paiute*, that "when blind people play, the *siki'ba* guesses are qualified by adding one of the cardinal directions according to the position [i.e. east-west or north-south] in which the players are seated." Also, when the guessing is down to just one pair of bones, *"ka'su'kwan"* and *"tasi'güwai"* are the guesses, not *"siki'ba."*

the other team would take its turn, and whoever had the most counter sticks left would be the first to hide the bones in the real game. These days, the toss of a coin often decides.

Next, two players on the successful side hide the bones as the other players on their side sing hand-game songs. When they indicate that they are ready—each player refines the basic gestures in his or her own style, but basically the hands stop moving back and forth—a player on the other side guesses, using specific words and gestures to indicate one of four possible combinations. Imagine that the players hiding the bones are sitting side by side. The combinations are: plain bones in their outside hands; plain bones in their inside hands, that is, the hand of each player that is next to the other player; plain bones in right hands; or plain bones in left hands (see "Guessing" on the opposite page). The music continues as the players reveal the locations of the bones. If the guesser was right about both sets, the bones go to his or her side, which starts a song and begins to hide the bones. If one guess was right, that pair of bones goes to the guesser's side, but the player who successfully hid the bones hides them again, and the guesser's side forfeits one counter stick. If both guesses were

BONES

Hand-game bones made from the leg bones of mountain lions and mountain sheep used to be common. Eagle wing tubes were used, and according to at least one account, Wintu people considered bones made from coyotes to be particularly powerful, since Coyote was the "patron" of Wintu gambling.

Deer leg or wooden dowels are the norm these days. Deer sinew or string made from Indian hemp or milkweed might be used to wrap the marked bone, while "bones" made of wood might instead have a band cut or burnt into them. Rumsien Ohlone players once used strings of olivella shells in place of bones, and Surprise Valley Paiutes (and probably others) used strings of beads. At one time, Mono hand game was played with strings of dyed acorns. Later, it was played with two strings of beads: both had four white beads, and one string had one blue bead while the other had two.

To make contemporary, Sierra Mewuk-style hand-game bones, start by removing the hide from the foreleg of a deer (doe or buck). Saw off a three-inch section of bone, and remove the rough edges left from sawing by filling them in, grinding them, or rubbing them smooth on a rock. Next, boil the bones to remove marrow and oil. Mark one of them by wrapping a length of dark string around the middle until the wrapped section is about half an inch wide. Attach the string permanently with pitch, soaproot glue, or a similar adhesive.

Hand-game bones range in length from about an inch and a half to four inches, the idea being that they can be hidden comfortably in the palm of one's hand. Some bones are hollow, and some are filled with pitch. I've been told that the reason for filling them is to keep out the other side's luck, so if your bones aren't filled, blow through them before hiding them.

wrong, the guesser's side forfeits two counter sticks and the other side hides both sets of bones again. (By some accounts, a side gets the bones *and* a counter stick for each correct guess, but this is unusual.)

The total number of points, and hence counter sticks, in a game varies from one tribe to the next—eight, ten, twelve, and twenty are the most common. At the beginning of the game, teams take sticks from a common pile in the center, or an "umpire" hands them out. The Sierra Mewuk people call this person the fire tender, and it is an honored position because this person is dependable enough to settle disputes fairly throughout the long game, and to keep the fire going throughout the night. When all the sticks are gone from the center, the teams take them from each other as they gain points. When one team has all the sticks, the game is over. It's very simple, but infinitely entertaining.

At any moment, there are only three primary players—one guessing, and two hiding, but any number of people can be on a team, and the teams don't have to be the same size. Often, a leader for each team decides who will hide the bones and who

POMO GUESSING

In the old way of playing the Pomo grass game, players alternately move their right and left hands from front to back until they are ready for a guess, when they stop, both players with the same hand in front. The words for the guesses indicate which bones are in front. "Weh" is a guess that the marked bones are in front, and "dep" is a guess that the plain bones are in front. "Ko" guesses that the two plain bones are in the center, one in front and one in back. "Tule" guesses that the two marked bones are in the center, one in front and one in back. This is also true of the Wappo game (and probably others), although the words are a little different.

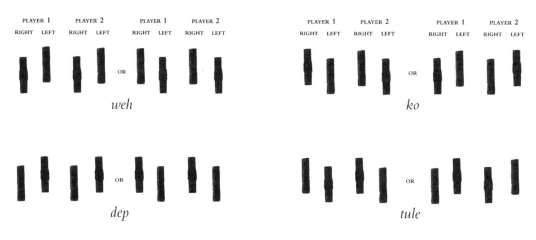

will guess. There aren't any set rules for when the bones change hands within a team; if a player is having bad luck the leader might decide to pass them to someone else, but maybe not. In some of the older versions, there is a specific procedure. For instance, if someone guessed where you were hiding them twice in a row you might pass the bones along, or they might automatically pass to the next player at each successful guess.

PEON

The game of peon is slightly different, both in the equipment and the manner of play. Each player has two playing pieces. One, often made of bone, is white, and the other is a dark piece of wood. Each piece has a cord attached to it, and each cord has a loop at the end so the player can slip it over his wrist. There are also counter sticks, the number varying from one tribe to the next. Here is an excerpt from an 1888 description of a Luiseño game:

> …The point in the game is for one side to guess in which hand of each player of the other side the white bone is. The sides arrange themselves

Young players learning peon at a fiesta on the Pala Reservation (Cupeño & Luiseño) in 1911. Photo courtesy of the San Diego Museum of Man, No. 1120.

Top left: a peon game at the Mesa Grande Reservation (Kumeyaay) in 1907. Players have hidden the bones. At right, the guess has been made and they are showing where the bones were hidden. Photos courtesy of the National Museum of the American Indian, Nos. 24288 and 24290. Below, players at the Pechanga Reservation (Luiseño) in the 1960s echo this gesture. From left to right, players are Eddy Salgado, Leroy Salgado, George Smith, Billy Salgado, and Joe (Cotton) Salgado. Photo by Ralph Michelsen courtesy of the San Diego Museum of Man, No. 24244.

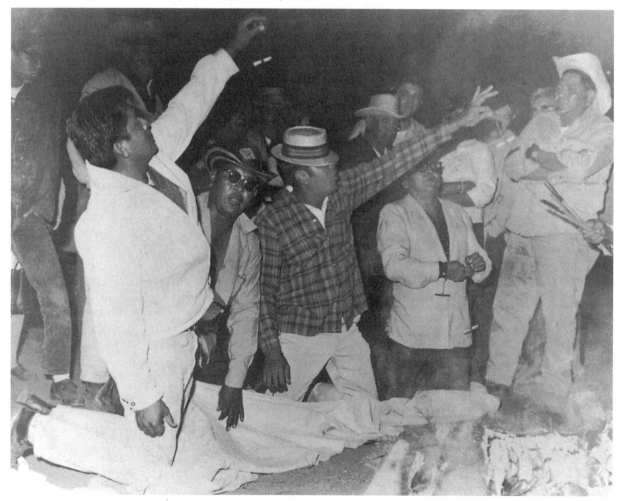

opposite each other. They toss to see which has the innings. The umpire gives the bones to the successful side and commences to sing. The [women] of each side arrange themselves behind the players; all are kneeling or sitting on their feet. Each side has a blanket stretched in front of their knees. The players having the bones grasp the side of the blanket in their teeth; it thus forms a curtain, and behind it they slip the [cords] over their wrists, without the opposite side seeing which hand the white bone is in. As they take the blanket in their teeth they join in the song with the umpire, swaying their bodies and making all sorts of grimaces with their faces. The women sing and keep time with them. The opposite side watches every motion, chatter and talk to each other, and the game becomes exciting as the four drop the blanket from their mouths and join in the song, in a louder key, with the women. They have their arms crossed, with their hands under their armpits. The other side at once commences making all sorts of motions at them, pointing to each one, sometimes with one finger, then two, when finally one of them announces which hand the white bone is in of each of the four.... If they only guess one or two, then the ones they have not guessed go through the same motions until all are caught, when the other side takes the bones, and the performance goes on until one side gets all the counters, and the game is ended with a regular jubilee... of the winning side. The umpire, who has watched the game all through and whose decision on any disputed point is law, hands over the money to the winners, who are nearly exhausted, for it takes from three to five hours to play the game.

Doctor Palmer, 1888 (in Culin, Games of the North American Indians)

As in hand game, the side that is hiding the bones gets a counter for each mistaken guess; if four players hide bones and the other side makes four bad guesses, the first side gets four counters. If the other side makes only one bad guess, the first side gets just one counter. Peon is still popular today, a much-anticipated feature of southern California gatherings.

INDIAN CARDS

In northwestern California, "Indian cards," sometimes called the "many-stick game," was and still is the preferred version of hand game. This game is also about hiding and guessing, but instead of sets of two bones, players use sets of slender sticks ranging in number from about fifty or less to a hundred. All the sticks are plain except a few, maybe four, which are marked with bands around their centers. Although there are several of these "aces," only one is used at a time. As in other, similar games, songs are an essential part, and northwestern players have a distinctive, rectangular style of drum.

To play, the "dealer" holds the sticks behind his back, dividing them into two bundles, one with an ace in it. He brings the sticks forward, and one of the players on the other side guesses which hand holds the ace, by clapping and then pointing to the hand he thinks *doesn't* hold the ace. The dealer then starts dropping sticks from his other hand (the hand not pointed at), and if the ace appears, the guessing side gets the deal. If the guess is wrong, the dealer's side gets a counter stick. Teams do not always specify who will be the guesser, and if two people from one side happen to guess at the same time, the dealer's side wins the point. Usually, the leader of a side has the first deal, but as the game progresses he chooses other players to take his place.

The sticks are about nine to ten inches long, sometimes tapered at the ends and sometimes blunt. Of the northwestern California sets described in *Games of the North American Indians*, the number of sticks in a pack ranges from 8 to 250, the number of aces ranges from 1 to 8, and the proportion of aces to sticks is anywere from about one in eight to one in fifty, with no correspondence to the total number of sticks in the pack. Very often, the sticks are simply peeled and not decorated except for the aces, which have a plain black band painted around their centers, but sometimes decorations are more elaborate. Culin described a Yurok set he collected in 1900 as "set of ninety fine splints, stained yellow, four marked with black in the center, ten with black spiral in center, and ten with black spiral at the ends; length 9-1/2 inches. Eleven plain splints in the bundle are 8-3/4 inches in length." The game is usually played for 11 points.

An Atsugewi Version

In other parts of northern California, even where hand game is played, many-stick game probably predated it and was of tremendous importance, as this description of an Atsugewi game reveals:

> This, *júpow montaiwas* (big gamble), was the biggest game of all in respect to the amount of property wagered. Each side bet all its property, which was piled high on both sides. One game settled everything and might last four or five days and nights…. Equipment included twenty-four to fifty slender willow sticks about ten inches long and a small ace three or four inches long, pointed at both ends and having a black band around the center. The dealer, who led the singing for his side, separated the willow sticks into two bundles and secreted the ace in one of them. Then he carefully wrapped each bundle in grass and laid them down before him, sprinkling water on them for good luck. Individuals from the other side came over one

at a time and scrutinized the bundles, conferring to-gether afterwards. An hour or more might elapse before they announced their decision. The dealer picked up the designated bundle and shook out the ace if it was there; if it was not, the guessing side forfeited a counter.

Thomas Garth, 1953

Wintu, Nomlaki, Yuki

In northwestern California tradition, women watch Indian cards, but they don't play or sing. However, in some of the other northern California tribes, this was traditionally the women's gambling game. In Wintu country, for instance, east and slightly south of the Klamath and Trinity River tribes, men in 1935 were playing hand game, but women played *datcedope*, using a bundle of twenty to forty sticks about three to five inches long. The ace was marked by leaving a band of bark

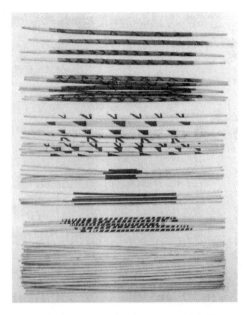

Yurok sticks for "Indian cards." Photo courtesy of the Hearst Museum of Anthropology, No. 17054.

A game of Indian cards at Blue Lake Rancheria (Yurok and Wiyot). The man with his back against the crates in the left foreground is hiding the ace. Photo courtesy of Humboldt State University, Susie Blake Fountain Collection, No. 941.

SONGS

Attending a big time or festival where people are playing hand game or Indian cards or peon is the best way to hear gambling songs, but readers might also want to check into some of the following sources.

A Guide to Cylinder Recordings (1900–1949) at the Lowie Museum of Anthropology, by Richard Keeling, published by University of California Press. In the late 19th and early 20th century, anthropologists from the University of California at Berkeley did extensive field work in California Indian communities.

Domingo (Yurok) with a drum for gambling. Photo courtesy of the Hearst Museum of Anthropology, No. 15-2713.

As a result, UC Berkeley's Hearst Museum of Anthropology (formerly the Lowie Museum) has significant collections of California Indian artifacts, photographs, and sound recordings. Sound recordings that were originally made on wax cylinders have been transferred to magnetic tape, and Keeling's guide, available through book stores and libraries, catalogs them. Readers interested in the music of specific tribes can then request cassette copies from the Hearst Museum, at 103 Kroeber Hall, University of California, Berkeley, CA, 94720.

Samplers: The Hearst Museum has made sampler tapes of their recordings. Tape #1 includes several Tolowa, Yurok, Hupa, and Pomo gambling songs, for instance. For more information, contact the Hearst Museum.

Some California public libraries, and the California State Library in Sacramento, have special "California Indian Library Collections" from UC Berkeley containing photographs, recordings, and written works about tribes in their areas. The Hearst Museum sampler tapes are included in these.

The American Folklife Center at the Library of Congress (Washington, DC 20540) also has cassette recordings of Native American songs that were originally collected on wax cylinders. Catalogs of the collection are available. The Archives of Traditional Music at Indiana State University have California Indian music, including gaming songs. Other museums with California Indian collections may have recordings as well. You will need an appointment to do research at most museums, since they rarely have enough staff to handle walk-in researchers in addition to their regular workload.

around the middle, or if the sticks were unpeeled, by peeling a band away from the center of the ace. The dealer held the bundle behind her back while hiding the ace, or under a cover of cloth or hide. Wintu men had a different many-stick game, *bohemtcus*, which was also played by the Nomlaki. As in the Atsugewi game, the ace, about three inches long and tapered at both ends, was rolled in a bundle of grass and slender rods about a foot long. Players usually hid the sticks behind their backs, but as George Foster points out in a description of the similar Yuki game of *alkuš-móltmil*, "a skillful player would flaunt his ability by doing it in plain sight of his opponent." And the Yuki players didn't use grass.

Shasta

Shasta women, north of the Wintu, played *ku'ig*, with fifty or sixty peeled sticks, all painted alike except for one with a red or black ring around its center. The sticks were about ten inches long and one sixteenth of an inch in diameter, the entire bundle about two inches in diameter. Here is a description of shuffling:

> In playing the game, the bundle of sticks is held in the right hand, rather nearer the upper end than the middle; the other end of the bundle being rested on the palm of the left hand. By giving the two hands a slow, circular movement in opposite directions in a horizontal plane, the individual sticks are twisted and shuffled among themselves very thoroughly. This being done for a few moments, the bundle of sticks is divided in two, one portion being held in each hand; and the opponent now has to determine in which of the two bundles the marked stick is contained.
>
> *Roland Dixon, 1907*

In the Shasta men's game, *ke'tapig*, there are fifteen to twenty spindle-shaped sticks, all decorated except two, plus seven counters. It is more like hand game than many-stick game, in that the dealer hides only one decorated and one plain stick at a time, in bundles of grass held behind his back.

> With such a set of sticks a small red stone is often kept as a lucky-charm, and also a tiny obsidian knife, which is used to cut up glow-worms with which to rub the sticks for luck. In making the sticks, much ceremony is observed. They are generally made by two men together, who, after strict continence for five days, go off into the mountains alone. Here they sing and pray, and are not allowed to eat meat or fresh fish, being restricted to a very little acorn-meal and dried fish. In eating, they have to eat out of small, well-decorated baskets, and may drink water only if mixed

with a little acorn-meal. On their return with the finished sticks, the men are obliged to remain continent for another five days, before using the sticks, and must during this time bathe frequently.

Roland Dixon, 1907

Dixon adds, "When a man is gambling, his wife must be very careful as to her food, eating only dry fish and acorns, and drinking only water in which some acorn-meal has been stirred." And also in regard to the Shasta game, Catherine Holt points out that counters were made new each time because everybody handled them, and that the men's and women's games were never "played commonly," though other games were played "just for fun."

This caution and ceremony, these restrictions, prohibitions, and charms, are not merely for the sake of cultivating luck as many of us think of it in 20th century America. Gambling and guessing games were played in the context of spirit and creation, and where they survive, this is still true. In cultures throughout the world, games figure in the most fundamental beliefs and stories, and in Native America they have not been separated from this spiritual context. California gambling stories are particularly beautiful. The Chumash Sun and Morning Star play a game of peon every year to see if there will be rain or drought. Some stories tell of epic games in the mythic past between culture heroes and gruesome, often man-eating, villains. Mewuk, Paiute, and Pomo heroes from mythic times saved their people in gambling contests that involved dodging stones or arrows in sequences and patterns reminiscent of hand-game strategies and guesses. Mukat, the creator of the Cahuilla people, and his twin brother, Tamaioit, tried to create light by creating animals to chase away the darkness—a cricket, another insect, a lizard, a black and white lizard, and a person. This failed, so:

> Mukat and Tamaioit then said they should have something to smoke to remove the darkness, just as medicine men smoke now to remove disease. They therefore planned to make tobacco. Mukat took black tobacco from his heart and Tamaioit brought forth a lighter colored tobacco. Next, they needed some way to smoke it, so they each brought forth another substance from the heart. Mukat's was dark, Tamaioit's was light. With this they made pipes. There were no holes in the pipes. Mukat then took a coal of fire from his heart to light the tobacco with. Now they were ready to smoke. Mukat filled his pipe first, held it up in the air, and inhaled.
>
> He then decided to play a trick on Tamaioit, so he handed his pipe to

him and said, "I am holding it up high," but he held it low, and in the dark, Tamaioit could not see it. However, Tamaioit was always suspicious of Mukat, so he reached low instead of high, as Mukat had expected him to do, and seized the pipe. Tamaioit then got his pipe and really held it that way. Mukat, thinking the same trick was being played on him, reached high and of course missed it. Therefore, Tamaioit claimed he was the wiser, because he could not be fooled.

Lucille Hooper, 1918

Certainly, this is a prototype for peon. Following is a Kashaya Pomo story that also goes back to the beginning of time, on a day when Coyote got the other animals involved in a gambling game.

The Coastal Animals Gamble with the Forest Animals

There was one old man who used to tell Coyote stories. However he never did like to tell them in summertime but rather he preferred to tell them in the winter. He used to call us children in order to tell the stories; he used to call us to the little house where he lived. When he did so, we went in to listen. But they say that it is dangerous to relate Coyote stories while sitting up. "You will all lie down," he would say to us, lying down himself. And only one, the main one, laid down [with him, i.e., his favorite]. Then he used to tell this Coyote story that I am about to tell—about gambling.

The coastal creatures and the forest creatures were the ones who were going to compete with each other. There was the abalone, there was the turban snail, there was the large chiton, the small chiton, the sea anemone, and the mussel. And the creatures from the forest were the crow, and the Steller jay, and the chipmunk, and the skunk, and the bear. Those are the ones who were going to play together.

Now the forest creatures were making plans. "Let's go down to the beach and call them out so that we can compete here against each other," said one. And then they did call them up. They started to gamble.

Now the abalone knelt down first. Having done so, he started to play. This, they say, is his song—gambling song:

> "Under the water, abalone shell
> Under the water, sobbing."

Now the crow started to play. He began to sing. This is the song of that one:

> "When I look back over my shoulder
> Bobbing, bobbing, I dance,"

he sang while playing. They were all laughing and shouting, feeling good, thinking they were going to win. But [the opponents] guessed him correctly too.

Next it was the turban snail's turn to play but his song was not good; it didn't even sound like a song:

> [A series of smacks]
> he was making while playing.
> [A series of smacks]

he was making while playing. Then they guessed him too.

The person on the other side started to play next—the Steller jay started to play. But I don't remember the song of that person—it was a pretty song. Then he was playing, feeling happy, shouting, laughing. They guessed him too.

And now on the other side, the large chiton began to play. This is that one's song:

> "The large chiton is the lord
> Of the small chitons crawling around,"

he said while playing. Like before, they were laughing and feeling good, intending to beat [the opponents]. Then they guessed him too.

Someone holds the bones, one black and one white, [hidden one in each hand]. [The opponent tries to] guess which one is held out in front. There are twelve sticks to gamble with [to keep score].

The chipmunk started to play next. This is the song of that one:

> "I am chattering around
> Mischievous little creature,"

he said while playing. They were laughing and yelling continuously, thinking that they were going to win. They guessed him too.

Next it was the small chiton's turn to start to gamble. However I don't know his song. But it was a good song too. He played—while singing he played. Then they guessed him too.

The skunk started to play next. This is his song:

"Skunk goes around with his tail in the air,"

he said while playing. While he was singing, they were feeling good—his friends—shouting and laughing. But, as before, they guessed him.

Now the sea anemone started to play. The one who used to tell this story used to say that that one was a woman. She also played. She had a pretty song but I don't remember it. She played as the others had, and they guessed her too.

Now the bear is going to start to play. That bear had been claiming that he was an expert gambler. Now he started to play while they were laughing and shouting, expecting to win:

"Under a manzanita, swoosh, swoosh, grunt,"

he was saying while playing. They, unexpectedly, guessed him too.

The next to play is the mussel—the one that is going to win. But I have forgotten the song of that one. He played and played, singing while playing. Unexpectedly, he got more sticks than anyone. Then they guessed him, but he already had most of the sticks.

That is all.

Essie Parrish, 1958

A game of stick dice in 1994. Photo by Malcolm Margolin.

Dice

Stripes and spirals, diamonds and dots—stick dice, and the games played with them, are simple, elegant, and lively. Besides stick dice, California tribes have dice made of walnut shells filled with pitch and tiny bits of shiny abalone; snail shells filled with tar; acorn caps filled with talc; discs of abalone or mussel; and knuckle bones from deer. Some of the most splendid baskets in California, the home of the finest and most intricate baskets in the world, are the trays used with shell dice.

In many parts of California, dice were for women, but there were exceptions. Among the Western Mono, men and women played dice, together or separately. Among the Nisenan, mostly women played, but men did too. Among the Owens Valley Paiute, one game of stick dice was for women, and another, which used the same dice but was scored differently, was for both sexes. Stick dice were exclusively for women in much of Pomo country, but among their neighbors, the Wappo, men sometimes played. Yuki men didn't play dice in the old days, but started around the 1920s. Men played in some Yokuts groups, but not in others. In many places today, both men and women play.

Chumash Dice

The southern California coast from about San Luis Obispo to Ventura is the home of the Chumash people. It was about 1912 when Fernando Librado, a Chumash man born on Santa Cruz Island, showed the linguist J.P. Harrington how to play *pɨ*. Librado explained to Harrington that the game was sometimes used by the *'antap,* the secret society of Chumash leaders that presided over ceremonies, to settle questions about who would be *kwaiyin,* their leader, or who would succeed members who had died. Harrington wrote:

> The game of *pɨ* is played with walnut shells; women also play this game. Three wild walnuts were gathered and their shells split into halves, removing the meat from each. You thus have six half shells. The back of the

nutshells in considered "black," and the flat side of the shell is "white."

The 'antap divide into two sides, each side with six men. Each side has a man they have selected to be their candidate for the office of kwaiyin. The two candidates will play the pɨ game, sitting on their legs and facing each other with a flat basket between them. One player then asks the other: "Odd or even?" Before the game begins they come to an agreement that one candidate is for odd while the other is for even.

To show me how the kwaiyin is selected, Fernando and I will now play the pɨ game. He has previously decided to take odd, while I have even. The game begins with Fernando placing the shells on a table. He then picks up one of the shells and holds it tightly in his hands and, crossing arms with the nut in one of his hands, he sings the following song:

Hayononu hayohununo (6 times)
Ha ha ha.

I guess his right hand. He opens that hand but the nut is not there; I have lost. This means that Fernando has first play in the game.

Fernando picks up all of the shells and shakes them in the hollow of his hands held together. Then he tosses the shells on the table. Five of the six shells land with the flat side up. One shell lands on its side and therefore does not count. Fernando calls odds and picks up all six shells into his hands. He shakes the shells again and tosses them on the table. Only two shells land with flat side up. Again Fernando picks up the shells, shakes them, and makes his third and last toss. The shells land with five facing up. I win.

Harrington won the point because the *total* number of dice that landed flat side up during Librado's three throws was even. If, on the other hand, only four shells had landed flat side up on the last throw, Librado would have won the point.

Tongva

Just south of the Chumash, the Tongva people (sometimes called Gabrielino) had another intriguing dice game:

Another game called *chachaukel* was played between two. The counters consisted of fifty small pieces of wood, stuck on end in the ground in a row, and two inches apart, with a pointer for each player to show his stage of the game. Eight pieces of split reed, with the under side blackened, were thrown, points down, and as many white sides as came up, counted to the thrower;

but where all came up black, they counted also. To throw eight entitled the player to another throw.

The adversaries counted from opposite ends [of the line of counters stuck in the ground] and if one's count came to that of the other, the rule was for the party caught to commence anew; which prolonged the game sometimes to a great length.

Hugo Reid, 1852

Sierra Mewuk, Nisenan

There are six dice in the Sierra Mewuk game. To make them, you need three black walnuts, split in half. Take out the nutmeats, clean out the insides of the shells, and use the oily nutmeats to polish the outsides. Then, carefully fill the shells with melted pine pitch, with some charcoal mixed in to turn it black. You can add beads or pieces of abalone to the pitch, flush with the top, for decoration. You will also need ten counters. These are slender sticks, all of the same length (about ten inches long) and diameter (one quarter of an inch or less). They can be made of willow or chokecherry, picked in the spring or fall when the bark is easiest to peel off and then left for a year to season. You can decorate the counters by burning or cutting patterns into them.

Mewuk-style walnut shell dice and counter sticks made by Lucy Parker in 1994. Photo by Malcolm Margolin.

Traditional Sierra Mewuk players toss the dice on a basketry tray, but a piece of hide or cloth will also do. Start with all the counters in the middle. The first player throws the dice, and takes one counter stick if three dice land with the pitch side up. The only other way to score points is to get six up or six down, which is worth two counter sticks. Whenever a player scores, she gets another throw. Once all the counters in the middle have been picked up, the players take counters from each other as they win points. Whoever ends up with all ten counters wins, but it's not over until someone wins two out of three games.

Mewuk dice, and sometimes those of Mono and other Sierra foothills people, were also made by filling acorn caps with talc, the soft mineral from which talcum powder is made. In a Nisenan game, players might use two acorns, split lengthwise to make four dice, with the outsides scraped and painted red or black. They make a small bet at the beginning of each round. If the four dice land with two painted sides up and two down, it is worth one point. If all four land with the same side up it counts for four points. Each score earns another throw. After everyone in the game has had a turn, the one with the most points gets the stakes.

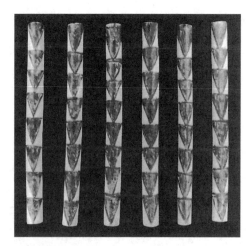

Pomo women's gambling staves. Photo by Scott Patterson, courtesy of the Grace Hudson Museum.

Pomo

Stick dice, sometimes called staves, were and are popular in many parts of California. Pomo stick dice are made of pieces of wood (often willow or elder) split lengthwise:

> Tree limbs, eight to fifteen inches long and one to two inches in diameter, are cut with the bark intact, and a halfway mark cut through the bark and into the wood around the length of each branch. Having divided each stick into sections, a design is cut out of the bark, one on each side. The stick is then held over a fire and the designs slowly burned into the exposed wood. The remaining bark is removed and the stick is left to "cure" in a dry area, free from direct sunlight. The curing prevents the stick from bending, especially when it is finally split. Having cured properly, the stick is split along the halfway mark. Three branches so treated yield six staves, each with a rounded and designed side and a flat and undecorated side.
>
> Along with the six staves, twelve counters are also used in the game. The counters, eight to twelve inches long and one quarter to one half inch in diameter, are made from hazel, ash, and dogwood. For the most part, counters are undecorated except for removing the bark.
>
> Although some people today make staves in the traditional way, many purchase half-rounds of redwood, pine, birch, or maple, cut them to the desired length, and create designs on the rounded half using an electric wood-burning iron of the type found in many hobby or toy stores. Counters are often made from commercially produced wooden dowels.

> *David Peri (Bodega Miwok), 1987*

This game is scored like the Sierra Mewuk game of shell dice described above: if three staves land with the rounded ("black") side up, it counts for one point; if all six of the black sides or the white sides turn up, it counts two points. As in the other games, players keep the sticks when they get points; if not, the dice pass to the other side. This game can be played by individuals or in teams, and it is useful to have a referee to call "black" or "white" if a stave lands on its side. The first side to get all the counters wins the game and the bets.

Elsie Allen (Makahmo Pomo) once told a story about stick dice that illustrates one of the roles of games in native California cultures, that of settling disputes. The story takes place near Cloverdale, before Europeans arrived in California. Two families had gone fishing for salmon together, and a dispute arose over how the catch was to be divided. They couldn't settle it, and went home with bad feelings about each other, which soon spread throughout the community as family loyalties came into play.

This thing carried on until acorn-picking time. After each family had gathered up its acorns, the headman said there was to be a big time and some people from different places had been invited; he had sent out his people to invite those others.

STAVES

Some stick dice are decorated on the flat side, and some on the round side. Some are painted and some have designs burned in. Tribes have their own traditions, and they work with the materials that are readily available to them: elder, willow, cane, palm leaf ribs, and cottonwood are a few possibilities.

 Two from a set of four Mojave stick dice, 5-3/4 inches long, 2-1/4 inches wide, painted on the flat sides in four different designs.

 Two from a set of four Quechan stick dice, 6-1/2 inches long, 1-1/4 inches wide, with four different designs painted in red on the flat side, and painted solid red on the rounded side.

 Two from a set of four Mojave stick dice made of willow, 6 inches long, 1-1/2 inches wide, painted with four different designs in brown on the flat side.

 One of four Quechan stick dice, 6 inches long, 1 inch wide, all painted differently in dark brown on the whitened flat side.

 One of six Pomo dice, 11 inches long, decorated on the rounded sides, all marked alike.

 Pomo stick dice. Length, 12-1/2 inches, decorated on the rounded sides, all marked alike.

 Pomo stick dice. Length, 17 inches. Set of 6, flat on one side, curved on the other, decorated on the rounded sides with burned designs in two slightly different patterns.

 Cahuilla staves of midrib of palmetto, 16 inches long, one side rounded, the other flat with burned marks.

 Cahuilla stick dice, 15 inches long, with incised lines on the flat sides. All four in the set are marked differently. The count is determined not by the marks, but by the number of flat sides up.

 Four Kumeyaay stick dice, 3-1/4 inches long, 7/8 inch wide, marked on the flat sides with burnt lines. In this case, the score is determined by the marks.

Drawings adapted from *Games of the North American Indians.*

Mojave women playing dice. Photo courtesy of The Huntington Library, San Marino, California (No. Pierce 02500).

The headman was upset about the bad feelings those two families and their relatives had for each other. He went to the two families and said, "This can't be any more this way; soon all of the people in the town will feel your way, and then nothing will be right; everything will go wrong. You people must settle this thing before those other people come here. I have talked with everybody; and they have put up many beads for the women to play for. The family that wins the game has the beads and loses their bad feelings. Those who don't get the beads win their good feelings back, and the other side will give some beads too because they feel good now that everything will be right again. It will be this way between you two families." This is what the captain said to those families. He put up a big feed for all the people after those families gambled and settled their bad feelings for each other. That's how my mother said the captain acted, one of the things he did in those days.

Owens Valley Paiute

In the Owens Valley Paiute women's game, there are 8 dice and 32 counters. The dice are made of pieces of cane split down the middle, with the inside surfaces painted red and the rounded, outside surfaces left white. To start the game, the counters are stuck in the ground in a semicircle, and players on each side either throw four of the eight dice or bounce them off their knees. Whoever has the most white sides land facing up gets to throw first. From then on, each white side that lands up is worth one point, except that if all eight dice land white side up, it's worth sixteen points. (By some accounts, having seven land white side up is worth fourteen points.) Each player has a marker, which she moves along the semicircle of counters according to the number of points she gets. Twice up and twice back, or 128 points, wins the game. In another Owens Valley game, the players—men and women—sit in a circle, one after the other throwing the dice. The only way to get a point is to have the dice land with one white and seven red sides up. This earns another throw, and four points win the game.

Mojave, Quechan

The beautiful Mojave and Quechan dice are made in sets of four, by splitting six-inch lengths of cottonwood *(Populus fremontii)* in two, lengthwise, and painting them with reddish-brown patterns, using mesquite gum *(Prosopis spp.)* dissolved in water. To start, players decide whether the plain or the painted sides will count, setting one of the dice down in the chosen position. Then a player throws the other three, and scores only if all three land in the same position as the first.

Yokuts

The people who have come to be called Yokuts lived in the San Joaquin Valley and adjacent foothills, from Mount Diablo in the north to the Kern River in the south. This huge group was made up of at least forty tribes, each with a distinct dialect and political autonomy. They played with stick dice and with shell dice, and the trays they used (a few of which are shown on the next page) are among the finest California baskets.

Walnut shell dice were just for women in some Yokuts tribes. In others, they were mostly for women, but men played too. Anna Gayton described the way Wukchumne women played around 1925.

> In playing, the dice were gathered in both hands cupped together, raised about two feet above the tray, and cast not directly downward but with a slight sideward movement. As the dice left the hands of an adept player, she clapped her hands together, and briskly waved the right hand as closely as she dared over the settling dice. This stereotyped gesture was theoretically supposed to fan the dice into falling in the preferred direction.

78

Top, left: Yokuts women with gambling trays. Photo courtesy of the Bancroft Library, University of California. Bottom, left: Yokuts gambling trays. Photo courtesy of the Southwest Museum (No. N-40037). This page: Louisa Francisco of the Tule River Reservation with a gambling tray she made, about 1910. Photo courtesy of Jeff Edwards.

There were usually eight dice, but scoring changed from one tribe to the next. The following table shows how many points would be earned by throwing walnut shell dice with 0 to 8 filled sides up, in five Yokuts variations of the game.

	Points				
Filled sides up	Tachi	Wukchumne	Kechayi	Choinumni	Yaudanchi
0	4	4	4	0	0
1	0	0	0	0	0
2	1	1	1	1	1
3	1	0	1	0	0
4	0	0	0	0	0
5	0	1	1	0	2
6	0	0	1	0	0
7	0	0	0	1	0
8	3	4	4	0	0

Taking all these variations into account, and the amount of interaction that must have taken place between tribes, it seems likely that the rules for scoring dice often had to be established at the beginning of the game.

"REMAINDERS" AND "MATCHING LINES"

Here are two other gambling games that can be fun, as well as mentally challenging. In "remainders," Pomo men started with 35 to 40 sticks about three inches long made of wormwood *(Artemisia ludovicia)* or California lilac *(Ceanothus* spp.), and either eight or twelve counters. Everyone put up something of equal value for the stakes. Then, a player would take a bunch of the sticks in his hand, holding it out in front of himself. The other side would try to guess whether, once the sticks were dropped in groups of four, the number remaining in the player's hand would be odd or even. If, for example, there were fourteen sticks in the bunch, the correct guess would be "even," because there would be three groups of four, with two sticks, an even number, left over; if there were fifteen sticks in the bunch, the correct guess would be "odd." In the Wappo version of this game, there are about fifty sticks, and the guess is based on the remainder after multiples of eight (instead of four). In the Nisenan game, the sticks are counted off in threes, and opponents bet on whether there will be one, two, or three sticks left over.

Matching lines: In this Mono men's game, two men face each other, holding basket trays on edge in front of them. With his index and middle fingers, one player draws a pair of lines in the dirt, from the edge of tray toward himself. One of the lines is longer than the other. The guesser tries to draw matching lines, hoping that when they move the baskets out of the way, his long line will be revealed to be on the same side as his opponent's. There are ten counters and a player receives one for each correct guess. One player continues to guess until he makes a mistake.

In a similar game from northeastern California, played also in parts of Oregon and Washington, a player arranges two short and two long sticks beneath a basket tray, and his opponent guesses, by making specific gestures with his fingers, how the sticks are arranged.

In the Tongva (Gabrielino) and Fernandeño game of *wauri*, one player arranges eight pieces of reed, painted on one side and plain on the other, behind a tray. The player on the other side draws marks in the dirt that correspond to the painted and plain sides, trying to duplicate the arrangement.

In a Yokuts version, two teams of four players each sit opposite each other. One man on each side holds a tray in front of his right hand, and they simultaneously make marks in the dirt with the three middle fingers of their right hands. Some of the marks are longer than the others, and these are the allowable configurations:

$$\mathsf{I_{II} \quad _{I}I_{I} \quad _{II}I \quad _{I}II \quad II_{I} \quad I_{II} \quad III}$$

If the guessing side fails to duplicate the opponent's marks, the opponent takes the pot. Traditionally, a player would pass the tray along to the next person when he got tired of making marks.

GAMBLING AND GAMING

As I write, any discussion of contemporary Native American games inevitably turns to casino gambling. As sovereign nations within the United States, tribes can conduct certain activities in Indian country that are not necessarily legal elsewhere. Throughout California and the U.S., there are tribes that have chosen to take advantage of this aspect of their sovereignty, building casinos that feature high-stakes bingo and other games, and attracting tourists to the reservations in droves, along with their money. Sometimes the money goes to good use—an East Coast tribe recently donated millions of dollars from casino earnings to the National

The Rumsey Rancheria's Cache Creek Casino, near Brooks, California. 1994 photo by Michelle Vignes.

Museum of the American Indian, for instance. On the other hand, some reservation communities have experienced the kinds of crimes that occur when a lot of money is involved.

While many Americans believe that gambling is a way of getting money for nothing, and that there is something wrong with that, there is no such stigma in California Indian tradition. When Charles Voegelin asked a Tubatulabal man if bets were wagered on their shinny game he was told, "Certainly they bet; they wouldn't run on a hot day for nothing!"

In native California tradition, to gamble well requires great skill and acuity, and the strength of character needed to cultivate power or luck is no small thing. Traditionally, players often underwent dietary and sexual restrictions to cultivate luck, sometimes using charms that were considered so dangerous, for example, that men with families wouldn't use them for fear of harming their children. There are also plenty of old stories about compulsive gambling. A tradition that embraces gambling while warning against excess will, perhaps, prepare people to face this challenge successfully. Here is the story of Mourning Dove, as Ray Baldy, a Hupa storyteller and language teacher, tells it:

> *Dong'who'dun* (long time ago), in legendary time, *Xonsil'chwiw* (Mourning Dove) lived in these times. He had a wife and several childen. Their home was in a village among friends and relatives.
>
> He was not a bad person or mean, but he had a bad habit. He liked to gamble. He began to go to other villages, looking for games. He traveled farther and farther from home and family.
>
> He neglected his wife and children. His wife tried to take care of the children and home as best as she could. Finally he wandered to a village several days' journey from home.
>
> He was gambling there when a relative caught up with him. The relative told him that his wife was sick and his children were suffering. He asked him to come home right away. He said, "I will come home as soon as I play this one more game." He finished the game and started for home.
>
> But when he reached home he found his home had burned to the ground. His whole family had perished in the fire. He began to mourn for his family and to this day he still mourns. That's why he makes that mournful sound: *Hi-yo-we-who'who… Hi-yo-we-who'who… Hi-yo-we-who'who…*
>
> *Hi'ya no:n dik* (that's the end, no more talking).
>
> *Ray Baldy (Hupa), 1994*

"A Warm Day," by Nellie McGraw—Hupa children swimming, ca. 1901-02.

No Batteries Required

Children's Games and String Figures

"Children's games consisted of imitating adult occupations (war, hunting, fishing, dancing)," wrote Edwin Loeb, describing the life of the Wailaki people in northern California in 1930. He went on to describe some of the ways in which Wailaki boys passed their time: throwing and dodging soaproot stalks and balls of sunflower leaves; advancing and retreating in lines, as in war, but shooting grass stalks from their bows; training to snare deer by rolling buckeyes into a net; attaching fish bones to the ends of sticks and using them to harpoon floating sticks in the river. "In May," Loeb concluded, "Boys put clover flowers in [their] hair [and] danced."

Engaged in the most universal of human activities—having fun—the children of native California learned how they would be expected to live. With the guidance of adults, they learned how to survive—how to hunt and fish and gather, and defend themselves in war. They began to learn the ceremonial singing and dancing skills that would keep the world intact. And as in this account of Nisenan childhood, they learned to live together.

> In the early days Indian children began early to make themselves useful. The old people taught them how to gather all sorts of things, to pick up acorns, to beat seeds, to pound. In conformity with that, the children played house. They made a little house. The boy said, "Let us two marry!" Then only two stayed in that little house.
>
> The little man went out hunting. The little woman pounded. She made mush out of mud. The little man came home from the hunt, he had some bark for a rabbit. The little woman said, "Eat that mud mush!" He said, "Well, the sun has gone down, let us sleep!" She said, "It is dawn," after sleeping a little. Then she said, "Let us eat mud mush, come on!" They

Northfork Mono girls with dolls in baby baskets. Photo by Nellie McGraw, courtesy of the Hearst Museum of Anthropology, No. 15-20939.

pretended to eat. The little man went to the river in pursuit of fish. He came carrying some leaves strung on string. The woman gave him mud mush. He said, "Roast the leaves!" She pretended to roast those leaves. They pretended to eat.

When the children grew older, the grown-ups made them a pack-basket and a seed beater. The grown people made a bow for the little man. He shot all kinds of small animals with that bow. The little woman went to their homes to get mush, and brought it to the play house. They roasted the small game that the little man had killed and ate that with the mush, sharing the food in their little house.

When they grew up together in this way and got used to each other, they usually married, the old people told them to marry, when they were used to each other; in this way those married who lived in the same camp. Then the parents gave each other valuables, that is the way they treated children who lived in the same camp, when they grew up. "That is good, let them marry, they got used to each other when they were small, go ahead!" they said.

William Joseph (Nisenan), 1930

Yes, the boys were doing most of the hunting and the girls were doing most of the cooking, in imitation of a division of labor that had served their families well for countless generations. But girls were not as constrained in their behavior as we might assume, nor did they lack training in survival skills.

We used to have wars against the boys [laughing]. I can remember how crazy we were. We used to have wars with them with *xamca·* (wild gourds), throwing them at each others' heads. We could have cut someone or put out each others' eyes. We didn't think about that then, we had so much fun. I've been hit many times in the head but we all had a good time. Sometimes boys and girls would be on both teams and other times it would

DOLLS

The Kumeyaay dolls in this photograph were probably made in the 1920s or 1930s. They may have been made for children to play with, or they may have been meant for sale to tourists. It's obvious that the women who made them were influenced by modern dolls, but the tradition of making dolls goes way back in Indian country. Remembering her Kumeyaay childhood in her autobiography, Delfina Cuero recalls making dolls of rags, stuffing them, and adding sticks for legs. They also made dolls of clay, which crumbled after a while because they weren't fired, and they made dolls of mud with stones for eyes.

Elsewhere, Cahto girls made dolls of deerhide rolled around sticks and carried them in tiny baby baskets made by their mothers. Pomo children made dolls of kelp, wild parsnip tops, clay, or wood. Sometimes girls would use leaves, especially madrone *(Arbutus menziesii)*, of all shapes and sizes to represent boys and girls, men and women, in plain or fancy clothes. Tubatulabal children used red clay to make

Kumeyaay (Diegueño) cloth dolls. Photo courtesy of San Diego Museum of Man, No. 2342.

"coyotes and also bears, wolves, and also people," Mike Miranda told Charles Voegelin in the 1930s.

You may come across photographs of striking, elaborately dressed clay figures from southern California, but don't assume that they are toys. Tribes in the Sierra Nevada and much of southern California made figures to represent the dead and burned them during mourning ceremonies.

be boys against girls. Sometimes it would end in a big fight and everybody would get mad. If someone got hurt we would be mad and have a real fight, but we were all right the next day—friends again. The gourds were round and hard, like hard balls. I can remember I used to get a licking all the time because I was always throwing things.

… We had a lot of fun with all kinds of games. We played hockey with a *wa·ta·š* (stick) and a ball and a goal. Our ball was made out of sticks. We shot bows and arrows and threw *xampu·* (rabbit sticks) at targets. My father made me a rabbit stick [a curved, flattened stick similar to a boomerang] but I wasn't very good with it. The older folks made little bows and arrows for us. Even the girls used them and learned to throw rabbit sticks. Some girls were good.

We used to make sticks for horses and ride those. We didn't have any toys to play with. We made our own things. We made play horses sometimes to play with. Even now, as old as I am, some days I'll be going and I'll see a puddle and bend down and make a face or animal's head in the mud. Just model in the clay. When I come back next time, if the rains came, I don't see it any more.

Delfina Cuero (Kumeyaay), 1965

CHILDREN'S GAMES

Here are a few traditional games. Some are universal and some unique, some still played and some ready to be rediscovered. Some of them are so simple and obvious that they hardly seem worth mentioning, but that's the point—children everywhere can have fun with the simplest "toys," given the chance.

In the Coastal Pomo game of *tcim*, a boy or girl would lie down in the sand and dig small holes in a line with a feather, calling out "tcim tcim tcim." The object was to see how far he or she could go without drawing a breath.

Dá tute is an Eastern Pomo game for young boys and girls, requiring only a ball made of tule fiber (*Scirpus* spp.), slightly smaller than a baseball. The players form a circle and someone starts the game by tapping the ball up inside the circle. As it starts to come down, a player who is close to it taps it up again. If a player misses or sends the ball out of the ring, he or she is out of the game, which continues until there is only one player left.

Chukchansi Yokuts children played a game that sounds very much like "London Bridge," but the woman who told ethnographer Anna Gayton about it said they had been playing it long before the arrival of whites:

Photo of Northfork Mono girls by Nellie McGraw, courtesy of the Hearst Museum of Anthropology, No. 15-20940.

This was played by girls ten to fifteen years old. A couple stood facing each other [and] clapped their hands together. Other children in line filed under the clapping arms, and the last in line was captured, if possible, by the couple. The one caught was then picked up by the feet and shoulders and swung back and forth until [s]he named [her] family's totemic animal. Those so caught were out of the game. When all were disposed of, the first couple was replaced by another pair. If boys played this game, they did so by themselves. It was a favorite at large gatherings...

Anna Gayton, 1940

The song that accompanied the game went "bala', bala', 'omis," translated as "clap, clap, mother." This was sung over and over, Gayton concludes, until the last in line, off guard, had been caught.

Here are Tubatulabal versions of tag and hide-and-seek, from Kern River country.

We used to play tag in the bull-pine trees. We would climb the trees and chase each other. We didn't play [this game] on the ground, but in the bull-pine trees. The one who was "it" would chase us. To catch us he touches someone. Then that one becomes "it" next. We would run away, up the trees. We would jump in different places in the branches of the bull-pine tree. Some would fall down and run away from the branches. Some would be hanging on the branches of the bull pines. We would play this during the day.

 … Then from there we are playing another game again, the hide game. Then we are putting one boy [to be "it"]. We are tying his eyes with a rag. Then he is seeing nothing. Then from there, having finished tying him, we are all hiding. Then he is looking for us. "Where are you?" he is saying. "This way," we are saying. Then he is coming running. Then some are coming in his tracks. Then he takes a jump backward. Then he is grabbing one boy. Then that one does the same next.

      Mike Miranda, also called Yukaya (Tubatulabal), ca. 1935

Marie Potts, a Northern Maidu woman, described games of her childhood in her book, *The Northern Maidu*:

> In one race, rocks were placed in succession along parallel lines, with one line of rocks for each player. Each contestant had to run to the first rock on his line and return it to his goal, then return with the next rock to the goal, and so on. The game was won by the first player to bring all his rocks to his goal.
>
> Another contest was one in which rocks were thrown, starting with small ones, and working up in size to big ones, until the rocks were too heavy to lift.
>
> Our children also had fun with supple young trees (saplings), pulling one down and riding it like a horse or swinging on it. Sometimes someone would take hold of the end and switch it from side to side, to see if he could buck the rider off.

This last game may have been fairly common in the days when the supply of saplings was inexhaustible: it occurs often in myth. In the following Wintu story, Sun and Tulchuherris, his son-in-law, play for keeps after a series of other contests:

> The next morning they got up and ate, then Old Man Sun said, "When people are young they like to play. I have a tree. I'll show you how to play on it." So, they went to the play tree and Young Fellow saw bones lying all around it. Sun said, "You climb up to that forked limb and I'll pull the fork

down." Young Fellow said, "I don't understand; you'll have to show me how to play." So the old man climbed up into the tree and Tulchuherris pulled the tree down and let it snap back. Then he climbed into the tree and let Sun snap him. Then Old Man Sun tried again but he went higher this time.

When it was Tulchuherris' turn he jumped down just before the tree snapped back. Old Man Sun did not see him and said, "Yes, Son-in-law, you think you are smart, you think you are smarter than I am." Then Young Fellow asked, "What were you saying?" Sun changed his tone and said, "I was just saying I thought I had killed a good man." They kept on doing this until they reached the top of the tree. Young Fellow said, "Now it is your turn, old man. I guess you had better climb to the top this time." The old man did not want to, but his son-in-law made him. Then he snapped Old Man Sun off into the sky. He saw drops of blood spatter down on the ground at his feet. Then he heard someone say, "Son-in-law, I thought I had more power than anyone else, but I guess you have more than I have." Then he said, "Send Gray Fox up here to me." So Tulchuherris threw Gray Fox up and Sun wrapped him around his head. That is why the sun has a gray haze around it. When Sun was snapped up into the sky he split in two, one half became the sun and the other half became the moon.

Jenny Curl (Wintu), 1929

Some simple toys based on human ingenuity and natural phenomena like gravity or sound waves occur all over the world, including native California.

Bullroarers

Tribes in the southwestern United States and elsewhere use bullroarers in ceremonies, and in some tribes they are also children's toys. By attaching a flat piece of wood about one by five inches to a long stick with a long (as much as three feet) leather cord, and then using the stick as a handle

Bullroarer drawing adapted from Games of the North American Indians.

while whirling the rest in circles above your head, you can create a powerful, buzzing noise. The Surprise Valley Paiute people made bullroarers of juniper, decorated with spots or lines. Sometimes they used them to make the wind blow, and sometimes as toys. Nearby, Atsugewi children were not usually allowed to play with bullroarers because for their people, bullroarers might bring sickness and misfortune.

RING AND PIN

A Wailaki ring-and-pin game. Photo courtesy of the Hearst Museum of Anthropology, No. 15-6628.

This game, common throughout North America and many other parts of the world, was not necessarily a children's game in California. Patwin women played it, Hupa men played, and Dr. John Hudson said that for young Pomo men and women it was "said to symbolize the desire for a partner."

The game usually consists of a ring or series of rings attached by a cord to a stick, and the object is to toss the rings out and catch them on the stick. Ring-and-pin games are a perfect reflection of the environmental, and hence cultural, diversity of what we now call California. Klamath River tribes used salmon vertebrae for rings. On the southern California coast, the Luiseño people used the large caps from Valparaiso acorns *(Quercus chrysolepis)*. In the Colorado Desert, Mojave players made the rings from small pumpkin rinds.

The Shasta people's version of this game, as described by Roland Dixon in 1907, adds still more to our understanding of native people's relationships with their environment:

The Shasta still play a game in which twelve salmon vertebrae are strung on a cord thirty or forty centimeters [about twelve to sixteen inches] in length, the end one being tied transversely to prevent the others from slipping off. The cord is attached to a slender, sharpened wooden pin about fifteen centimeters [six inches] long. The game consists in swinging the bones upward with a quick motion of the hand, and trying to catch as many as possible of the vertebrae on the pin. Each player tries five or six times, and the winner is he whose total of bones caught is the highest. The greatest skill is needed to catch the end vertebra, which has its openings at right angles to the others. Each vertebra is called a "moon," and by playing the game chiefly in winter, the moon is made to grow old quicker, and the winter thus shortened. The catching of the end bone, which is called the "eye of the moon," kills the moon, as they say, more quickly than catching the others. In winter, also, cat's cradle figures are made by the young people. These are made only during the waxing of the moon, the looping and stretching of the cord being supposed to hasten the growth of the moon. During the wane of the moon, on the other hand, the above-mentioned game of the salmon vertebrae is played, to hasten the moon's death.

Whirligigs

With a whirligig, you make a buzzing sound by pulling back and forth on a cord, causing an object strung on it to spin around. Stewart Culin describes whirligigs from Alaska to Montana, Arizona to California in *Games of the North American Indians*. His California examples are from Mono people in Madera County. One is made by wrapping a cord around the center of a deer's metatarsal bone, so that the cord extends out to both sides, with loops on the ends. The other has a two-inch pottery disk in the center decorated with red paint, with a continuous loop of cotton cord strung through the center. Bear River Athabascan children made acorn buzzers by stringing acorns on a cord made from the leaf fibers of native iris (*Iris douglasiana*), with knots between the acorns to keep them from slipping off. They played them by stretching the string out and gently bouncing the acorns on their teeth, using their lips and the size of the acorns to regulate the sound of the vibrations. Wintu children "played buzz," according to ethnographer Cora DuBois, "with an oval of bark in which two holes were made. Buckskin thongs were passed through the holes. The thongs were twisted and then held in either hand and pulled back and forth to produce a humming noise."

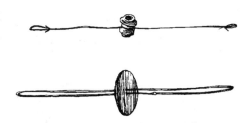

Deer knuckle and ceramic Mono whirligigs, and a wooden Yokuts top. Drawings adapted from Games of the North American Indians.

Tops

A deer once tried to pick up an acorn, but he missed it, causing it to whirl around. This is why Eastern Pomo children called acorn tops *bice ku tirltirl*, or "deer whirling about." Children and adults played with tops, made by inserting a small stick into the top of a whole acorn, then twirling it between two hands. The object was to see whose top would spin the longest after they let go.

Jacks

Three or four people at a time might play Paiute jacks, first gathering small stones in a pile, or placing them in a row, or hiding them in the dust. Then a player would throw a pebble into the air and grab as many stones as possible before catching the pebble. The person who got the last stone won.

Juggling

Atsugewi boys often juggled two rocks with one hand. Kumeyaay girls and young women also juggled with one hand—sometimes stones, sometimes pine nuts, small pumpkins or watermelons. They might start with two or three, and work their way up to seven at a time, switching hands when they missed. Among the Surprise Valley Paiute, women would juggle with three marble-like stones, betting against each other. One would juggle until she missed, and then it would be the next one's turn.

STRING FIGURES

Isabel Kelly, an ethnographer, once asked Piudy, a Surprise Valley Paiute man she was working with, about the juggling game. His response was, "That's no game; that's just for fun." Within the context of American mass culture, this is difficult to understand; if something isn't a game because it's "just for fun," then what on earth is a game for?

If it is connected to creation stories, a game can be a reminder of the laws and beliefs of the culture one comes from:

> Mukat [the Cahuilla creator] and his people lived in one big house. Animals were human then. They were all very happy here. Moon taught the people many games and they loved her very much. Every morning Moon took her people far away to the water and here they played all day long, returning to Mukat's house late in the evening.
>
> She taught them how to make things. "Cat's cradle" was one of the games she taught them. It was a game played by making figures by means of string twined around the fingers. There were many figures they had to know. Later when they died and went to Telmekish, they had to know how to make these figures and tell Montakwet, the guardian. If they could not do this, they were not admitted.
>
> *Lucile Hooper, 1918*

A gambling game also serves to move wealth around. A game might develop intuition, motor skills, memory, or imagination. It might be a good way to pass time among friends, settle a dispute, or get acquainted with strangers. String figures, often referred to as "cat's cradles," are a fine example of the multi-layered significance of games that appear at first to be simple pastimes.

No doubt children in many tribes played with string figures, but adults had many uses for them besides entertainment. Yokuts, Kumeyaay, and some other native Californian people used string figures to predict whether a baby would be a boy or a girl. Kumeyaay people also had a string figure for predicting whether or not a man would be bitten by a rat while out hunting. Some tribes predicted the weather with string figures, or even changed it. Shasta people played with string figures to encourage the moon to grow, hence passing the time and bringing winter to an end. According to George Foster in *A Summary of Yuki Culture*, the Yuki people made string figures just for fun.

String figures are a part of many Native American cultures, and of others throughout the world. The string figure known as "cat's cradle" is well-known in England

and many other parts of Europe, and probably came to them from Asia. Borneo, Korea, Australia, and Polynesia are all home to string figures. It is not unusual for identical figures to show up in distant places. Sierra Mewuk people, for instance, called the following figure a bark house. Yokuts people called it a sweat house with smoke rising, and the Yuki called it a rat house.

A Bark House

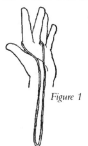
Figure 1

1. Start with a piece of string about six feet long that has been tied together to form a continuous loop. Drape the loop over the index and middle fingers of your left hand (Figure 1). Put your right wrist up through the other end of the loop.

2. With the thumb and index finger of your right hand, pick up the string between the index and middle fingers of your left hand, and bring it back to your right, letting the loop slip off your right wrist.

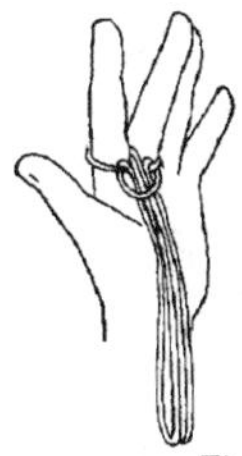

A bark house. Photo courtesy of the San Diego Historical Society.

3. Next, hang the loop over your right wrist again, and with your right index finger and thumb, reach between your left index and middle fingers. Pick up the two pieces of string you find there and bring them back to the right, again letting the loop slip off your right wrist. This will form a knot (Fig. 2).

Figure 2

4. At this point, there is a long, double loop between the knot and your right hand, with two strings on top and two strings below. Slip your little finger under the bottom string of the two that are closest to it. Do the same with your thumb, slipping it under the bottom string that is closest to it (Fig. 3).

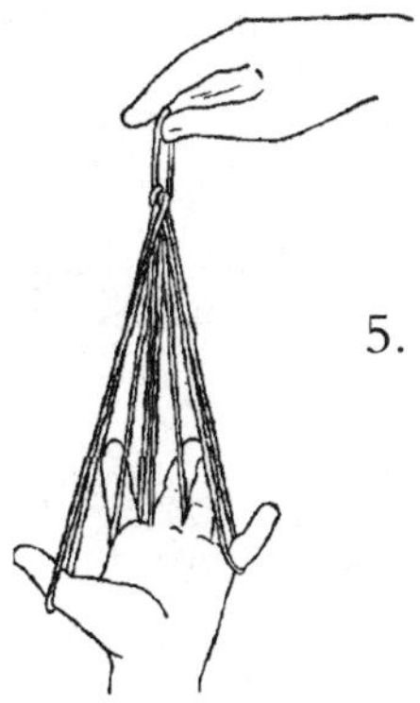

Figure 3

5. With your palm facing up, open out the fingers of your left hand, and drop the strings you are holding with your right hand. Pick up the knot with your right thumb and index finger, and gently draw it upwards. The result should look like Figure 4. A few quick, gentle tugs with your right hand will collapse it.

Figure 4

Diamonds

This figure used to be known as a deer snare to the Wailaki, but when George Foster described it in 1944, it was called "diamonds." Other North American tribes, such as the Osage, knew this one, and it also shows up in the Hawaiian Islands and Ireland.

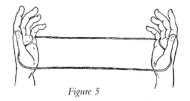

Figure 5

1. Again, start with a piece of string about six feet long that has been tied together to form a continuous loop. Put the thumbs and little fingers of both hands inside the loop, stretch your fingers out, and hold your arms apart (Fig. 5). Slip your right index finger under the string that is crossing your left palm and draw your right hand back. Slip your left index finger under the string crossing your right palm, within its intersection with the loop around your right index finger, and draw your left hand back (Fig. 6).

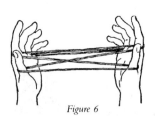

Figure 6

2. Drop the loops around your thumbs, moving your hands apart. Twist your palms away from you so that, on the backs of your thumbs, you can pick up the farthest string on the loop around your little fingers. Bring your thumbs back, so that the string travels under all the others.

3. With your thumbs, reach over the nearest string in the loop around your index fingers. Slip your thumbs under the farthest string in that loop and bring them, with the string, back to their original position (Fig. 7).

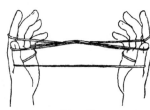

Figure 7

4. Drop the loops from your little fingers, moving your hands apart. With your little fingers, reach over the loop on your index fingers and, from below, pick up the side of the loop around your thumbs that is farthest from you. Return your little fingers to their original position.

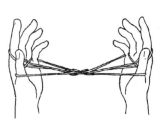

Figure 8

5. Drop the loops from your thumbs. With your thumbs, reach over the loop on your index finger, and from below, pick up the nearest string on your little fingers. Return your thumbs to their original position (Fig. 8).

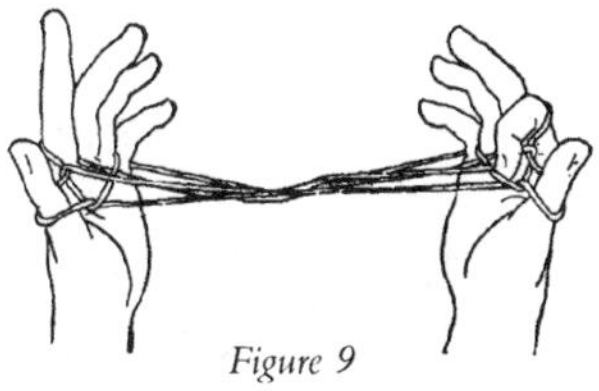

6. Use your teeth to pick up the loop on your right index finger, just where it comes off the finger, and draw it over your thumb as well. Do the same on the left side.

Figure 9

7. Below the loop you just added to your thumb, there is another one. With your teeth, lift this loop over the new one and drop it off your thumb. Do this on both sides.

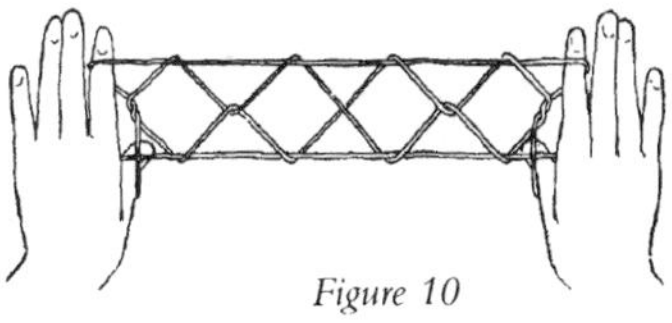

8. There should be a small triangle next to the loop around each thumb, formed by the string you just moved, the string crossing your palm, and the loop around your thumb. With both index fingers at the same time, reach into these triangles from above (Fig. 9, right hand), meanwhile dropping the strings off your little fingers, turning your palms away from you, and stretching your thumbs and index fingers far apart (Fig. 10).

Figure 10

String Your Fingers Up

This Yuki string trick is another one that appears all over the world—Africa, Japan, the Philippines, Ireland, and Sweden, to name a few places—as well as native North America, including Alaska. As is true with many string figures, part of the pleasure of doing it is developing a properly subtle but dramatic flair. It can be frustrating to follow written instructions, but this one is worth it!

MAKING STRING

Some of the many plants that string can be made from are milkweed (*Asclepias* spp.), Indian hemp, also called dogbane (*Apocynum* spp.), wild iris (*Iris* spp.), and yucca (*Yucca* spp.) Yucca and iris leaves are pounded to extract the fibers that will become string, or Spanish bayonet (*Yucca baccata*) leaves can be buried, so that the flesh rots away from the fiber. One way to extract fibers from milkweed and Indian hemp is to crush a dried stalk and then carefully peel the core away from the fibers in short sections. The next step in the process is to clean the fibers by rubbing them between your hands, as you would scrub laundry. Then, after being soaked, the fibers are twisted. The basic idea for strong, two-ply cordage is to twist the fibers in the two bunches that will become plies in one direction (e.g. clockwise), and then twist them around each other in the opposite direction.

Figure 11

Figure 12

Figure 13

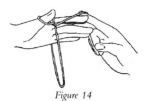

Figure 14

Figure 15

Figure 16

1. Again, use a piece of string about six feet long that has been tied together to form a continuous loop. This time, hold your left hand out with the thumb on top, and drape the loop over your whole left hand, including the thumb (Fig. 11).

2. Slip your right index finger into the loop, and reaching between your left thumb and index finger, grab the string and pull it back a little, in the direction of your chest (Fig. 12). Give this little loop a clockwise twist, so that the part that was on the bottom is on top and vice versa (Fig. 13). This is critical to the success of the operation.

3. Now take the loop away from you and hang it over your index finger (Fig. 14). Give the strings hanging down over the rest of your left hand a tug to tighten the loop.

4. Slipping your right index finger into the remainder of the loop on your left hand, reach between the index and third fingers of your left hand (Fig. 15) and do the same thing: grab the string, pull it back a little, twist it clockwise, and this time drape the loop over the third finger of your left hand.

5. Do the same thing with the ring and little fingers of your left hand. Each time, tighten up the loop by pulling the strings hanging from your left hand. It should look like the drawing in Figure 16.

6. This is where the dramatic flair comes in. Slip the loop off your left thumb and hold it between your left thumb and index finger. With your right hand, pull the string nearest you that is hanging off the bottom of your left hand, simultaneously letting go with your left thumb and index finger. The whole complicated assembly should come off with one good tug.

Mojave runners Simon Garcia and Augie Medrano in 1992. Photo by John Picone.

Racing for the Moon

Contests, Races, and Running

Fox was preparing to hunt. He named all the others who would be allowed to go along, and they all started to boast about their special skills. Mountain Lion would get into the hills before anyone else, and kill a large deer. Mountain Quail was the only one not afraid to go into the brush, where he would meet and kill a large deer. Wolf would chase a deer until he ran him down. Coyote, too, would chase the deer down—plenty of them—whether the ground was rough or smooth, and eat them while they ran. Crow could find more deer than anyone, even Eagle. Hummingbird, Dove, Brown Wren, Turkey Vulture, and Jay all had their special techniques. Skunk would kill the deer by spraying on them.

In this Sierra Mewuk story we find the sheer and simple joy of competition. Those mythic people at the beginning of the world didn't need sticks, rackets, hoops, poles, or arrows to compete with each other, and neither do we; each of us, given a chance, can find a talent to nurture, and thereby contribute to the well-being of the whole group. Thomas Garth's description of miscellaneous Atsugewi games enumerates some of the possibilities:

> Wrestling for stakes occurred, the best man from each of two sides competing. The man first succeeding in throwing his opponent down won. If a man lost, another man might take his place for the next bout. A wrestler might acquire a bullsnake spirit guardian, which resided between his shoulders and enabled him to squeeze hard. In another contest, the object was to carry a heavy rock over a line at some distance away. Again a rock might be pushed out from the shoulders as in our shot put, but differing in that a man could not move his legs or lean over as he propelled the stone.

The farthest toss won. Another test of strength was to try to pull a pair of deer horns apart. There was also a jumping game in which the contestants stood feet together and took two jumps, going as far as they could....

Thomas Garth, 1953

In Eastern Pomo wrestling matches, according to Edwin Loeb, "one man would place his hands in front of him for protection, while his opponent would try to trip him up and lay him on his back. When the man was down, the contest was ended." There was also a form that Loeb calls "Indian ju jitsu," in which two men stood at arm's length from each other and grabbed each other's little fingers, each trying to twist the other's hand. Yuki wrestlers would stand opposite each other, grab hold of each other's hands and arms, and try to throw each other to the ground. Wappo men wrestled the same way, though ethnographer Philip Driver noted another kind

Tests of strength and stamina are as popular in native California as they are in the rest of the world. Photo labeled "Cinon Duro and the lifting stone—Mesa Grande fiesta, 1903," by Constance DuBois, courtesy of the San Diego Museum of Man, No. 1017.

of match, in which two men would sit on the ground, legs outstretched and feet touching, each grasping one end of a stick, and pull against one another. The object was to pull your opponent off the ground.

Swimming races and diving contests were common. People dove to see who could go deepest or stay under water the longest. Yuki swimmers were said to swallow the airbags of suckers *(Cacostomidae,* native fish adapted to feed at the bottom of lakes and rivers) in hopes that they would improve their diving and breath-holding skills.

Children, of course, had their own contests. Nisenan boys would make small bets that they could jump repeatedly over a large rock. At first, all the players would be able to do it, but a winner emerged as the others got tired, stumbled, and left the game. Maidu children would mark a rock by wrapping a string around it, throw it in the river, and race to see who could retrieve it first. Pomo children played tag in the water as well as on land. This Yurok story may have been told to nudge young minds into recognizing the potential of even their least graceful peers:

Many years ago there was a total eclipse of the moon which lasted for several days and nights. The night continued so dark that the people and animals were not able to see to go about, so all the animals of the animal kingdom held a council and decided to devour the moon, as it had become a useless planet and would not give them light at night.

The animals journeyed from the earth up to the moon and began a fierce battle to conquer and devour it, and after a long struggle the moon lost its balance in the heavens and fell earthward. It struck the earth at Ca-neck on the Klamath River, where the waters whirl and rush into fearful rapids. At the lower terminations of these rapids, where there is a large round depression in the land, on the south and west side of the river, is the place where the moon is supposed to have struck the earth when the animals threw it down from the heavens.

While the animals and snakes were wrestling with the moon at Ca-neck, it was then the frog stepped forth and objected, saying that they should not devour the moon completely, as they would need it to light the world at night in the future. Listening to the frog's wise council, they all agreed to allow him to restore the moon to its proper place. So the frog began at once to gather all the blood of the moon and fuse it together with its other remnants, and when he had completed the task, all the reptiles and animals rendered their assistance in trying to throw the moon back into the heavens so it would shine again.

The great multitude of animals became exhausted in their mighty efforts, as they could not even move it from its resting place on earth. They were all so tired that they were about ready to give it up in despair, when the little ant *(hah-pooth)* came forward and suggested that he was able to do it. The multitude roared with laughter at the ant and taunted him with jeers, saying: "You little *hah-pooth*, what can a little insignificant thing like you do with the great big moon?" However, the little ant saw the opportunity to show his power of great strength, even if he was little, and rushed in among the crowd and made his way right under the moon. The moon began at once to raise from the earth, and with one mighty effort the little *hah-pooth* threw the moon back into the heavens where it has ever since remained.

Lucy Thompson (Yurok), 1916

Top: A Pomo ceremonial basket, decorated with clamshell beads and quail feathers, purchased in 1906. Photo courtesy of the Brooklyn Museum. As the detail shows, a player would most likely run out of breath before he or she ran out of coils (stitches).

Bottom: The roundhouse at Tuolumne Rancheria, like roundhouses in much of California, is a center for ceremonies, sweats, and socializing. 1994 photo by Dugan Aguilar.

People can find something to compete about in nearly any situation, so it is no surprise that many of the contests ethnographers have noted reflect specific aspects of native California cultures—intricate basketry, the camaraderie of the men's sweat house, or seasonal food gathering. Nomlaki festivities included a contest to see who could count the most coils of a basket while holding his breath. Pomo men, and probably others, had competitive sweats when visitors came to their villages. Competing sides would try to fan as much heat as possible over to the other side of the sweat house while the fire was still burning high. To leave the sweat house was to acknowledge defeat. When the flames died down the men would go outside for a quick swim, then come back in, and it was actually at this point, with warm air, smoldering embers, and wet skin, that the real sweating began.

Lucile Hooper describes what is perhaps the ultimate form of resourceful gambling in *The Cahuilla Indians:*

> The old men used to study the stars very carefully and in this way could tell when each season began. They would meet in the ceremonial house and argue about the time certain stars would appear, and would often gamble about it.... After several nights of careful watching, when a certain star finally appeared, the old men would rush out, cry and shout, and often dance. In the spring, this gayety was especially pronounced, for it meant that they could now find certain plants in the mountains. This was a cause for great rejoicing, for food was often very scarce in those days. They never went to the mountains until they saw a certain star, for they knew they would not find food there previously.

Lucile Hooper, 1918

In the midst of all this healthy competition, people were aware of the dangers of excess. The Tongva story of Coyote and Water is a perfect injunction against foolish self-absorption: Coyote came to the edge of a small river one day. Looking over the bank, he saw that the water ran very slowly. "How about a race?" he asked, looking sly. "All right," the water answered, very calmly. Coyote ran along the bank at full speed until he was so tired he could hardly stand. Then he looked over the bank, only to see the water running smoothly on.

RUNNING

> Antelope challenged Deer to a race, saying, "I can beat you running." Deer said, "I think not." They agreed that they would run for six days, and went far to the south, across Tulare Lake, so they could run northward to the end of the world. Antelope chose the path to the west, and Deer chose the path to the east. Their paths were on the Milky Way. On the side where Antelope ran there is a wide path; on the other side there are patches. That is where the deer jumped. Antelope had said, "If I win, all this will be my country and you will have to hide in the brush." Deer said, "Very well, and if I win it will be the same for me." Then they ran, and Antelope won. So now, he has the plains to live in, but the deer hides in the brush.
>
> *A.L. Kroeber, 1907*

This Tachi Yokuts story is one of many California creation stories that feature foot races. Like children everywhere, native Californians hopped, skipped, jumped, and especially ran through the first years of their lives. "On the night of the new moon," Lucile Hooper writes in *The Cahuilla Indians,* "The boy who first saw it would run and tell the other boys of the village. All of the boys would then race to a certain spot, often many miles away, where there was water. Here they would jump in and swim, and then race back home again. This was supposed to bring them good luck during the following month."

The idea of racing for the new moon is all the more poignant when we know that "Moon taught the people many games and they loved her very much," but she decided to leave when she learned that Mukat, the creator and her father, wanted her for his wife. She told the people that there were games she had not yet taught them, but it was too late:

> That night she left and got beetles and ants to crawl over her tracks so that no one would follow her. Everyone felt very badly and tried to find her. Coyote went to the water where they always bathed to look for her. He saw her reflection in the water and thought it was she. He jumped in after her but couldn't find her. When he climbed out and looked in again, he was sure he saw her and again he jumped in, with the same result. As he

came out this time, Moon, who had gone to the sky, spat on him. He looked up to see where the spit had come from, and he saw her. He begged her to return but she would not talk, only smiled. He then returned to the others to tell them where their beloved playmate and teacher had gone. He felt very sad, so he hung his head as he said, "Here she is, here she is." The people looked down where he was looking, but of course could not see. Finally someone happened to look up and there saw Moon in the sky. She seemed very far away and they all wept. Each night, for a long time, she went higher up, until she was where we now see her.

Lucile Hooper, 1918

Other Shoshonean children—the Acjachemem and Luiseño, for example—also ran for the new moon. And in the north, new Pomo fathers would carry their infants as they ran to greet the first full moon after the baby's birth.

Some children, as they grew older, found they had a talent for running, even a calling—for many tribes, running was a vocation resonant with spiritual overtones. In north central California, Nomlaki runners dedicated their lives to carrying messages.

Newsboys can carry news from Paskenta to Tehama and back between evening and dawn. It is about thirty miles each way. They trot. They have free passage into enemy territory. It is necessary that they eat special kinds of food which is more preserving to the Indian body. The runners have to be careful of their diet. They are from 25 to 40 years old, for they can't do this work when they are too young. They have to keep their wind. Special ones are picked for this—not just anyone. They try out on the plains—people say that this is the hardest place for runners.

The runner is in a dangerous position. He does no other work, for he must always be ready to go. When he isn't running, he practices. He doesn't hunt or fish, but is well taken care of. He gets paid for his trips wherever he goes and he accumulates quite a lot. Several people may pay him for one trip, and he might get as much as $75. There aren't runners at every village; they are pretty scarce. They are important for wars.

… After the runner comes back, after he catches his breath, he tells everything that was said. Two fellows repeat what he said, so that everything is heard three times. Everyone listens, and when they are all through they discuss the matter.

Jeff Jones (Nomlaki), 1936

Traveling among the Mojave in 1886, John G. Bourke heard stories of a runner who traveled nearly two hundred miles in less than a day. In the same region, writes Peter Nabokov in *Indian Running*, "the Cocomaricopas developed a highly regarded runner service which ultimately connected Arizona with California and Sonora, Mexico. The route was especially active toward the beginning of the 19th century, as Cocomaricopas and Halchidhomas carried news between San Gabriel, Mexico, Tucson and San Diego. Yuman runners were prized for the two qualities which all runner systems regarded as critical, endurance and reliability."

In *The Chemehuevis*, Carobeth Laird describes the group her husband, George Laird, knew in his youth as the Runners as possibly "the last remnant of an ancient cult or guild." One man in the group, Kaawɨʔa had a "secret way of travelling, which was the old way."

Early one morning, George Laird said, they were all in the vicinity of Muuviᵞa, Cottonwood Island, in Nevada. The sun had not yet risen. Kaawɨʔa stood up and announced, "I am going to Yuma"—that is, to the Chemehuevi settlement at the mouth of the Gila, near Fort Yuma. "We'll all go," his companions said. But when he answered, "No," quietly and firmly, they did not argue the point, for they knew what he had in his mind to do. They watched him run away from the camp in a long, easy lope and disappear over a sand dune, just as the rays of the rising sun struck across it. The young men were silent for a while. Then one suggested, "Let's track him." They followed his tracks up to and over the crest of the dune to the point where they had lost sight of him. The tracks continued on, but now they were different. They looked as if he had been "just staggering along," taking giant steps, his feet touching the ground at long, irregular intervals, leaving prints that became further and further apart and lighter and lighter on the sand. Silently, by mutual consent, the other Runners continued on down-river. When at length they reached the village at the mouth of the Gila, they inquired, "Did Kaawɨʔa come here?" "Yes," the people answered, "He arrived on such and such a day (the day that he had left them), just as the sun was rising."

No one ever saw Kaawɨʔa travel in his special way. If he happened to sight a party ahead of him, he would join them, running in the usual way, and go along with them at whatever rate they were travelling. No, George Laird said, he had no tutuguuvi, no supernatural helper; what he had was the ancient knowledge.

Carobeth Laird, 1976

Running was an essential part of the passage to adulthood for children of many California tribes. Washo, Maidu, Karuk, and Luiseño girls' puberty ceremonies were among those that included exhausting elements—some would say ordeals—that emphasized the seriousness of the occasion and the virtue, once again, of endurance. Pomo, Serrano, and Luiseño puberty rites for boys also involved running. Nabokov writes that during the nose-piercing rites for both Achumawi (northeastern California) and Yuma (Colorado Desert) boys, which took place when they were eight or nine years old, "they were taken on a northerly run of up to fifteen miles. For the next three days this was repeated to the west, the south, and finally the east, as if to integrate them, at this vulnerable moment, with the geography which would nourish them all their lives."

Running continues to be an important part of California Indian cultures. It was Karuk runners from northwestern California who in 1927 and 1928 came in first in the 480-mile Grant's Pass Run, from Sausalito, California to Grant's Pass, Oregon. After winning in 1928, Henry Thomas was called "Flying Cloud," after the car he won as first prize. And as we move into the 21st century, running has become a popular way for Native Americans to make environmental statements. Since 1981, the Sacred Run Foundation has sponsored annual runs whose purpose is "to carry the message of the sacredness of all things, our relationship with the Earth and all living species, and the need to maintain the delicate balance that exists between humankind and the Earth." In southern California, Native Americans have held "Spirit Runs" to publicize their objections to government plans to build a radioactive waste dump in Ward Valley, between the Turtle Mountains and the Old Woman Mountains. Steve Lopez, a Mojave advisor on the runs, started a 1992 run with this prayer:

> We burn this arrowweed for vision and for strength. Ward Valley is our home, the land of our people, the Aha Macav. We have been here from time immemorial and we can't just get up and leave. This nuclear dump they want to put in here is a threat to the plants and animals who live here. It is a threat to our water, and a threat to the future. Many different tribes trace their ancestors from here. It's important that we all work together, that all the tribes join to become strong. We take part in this Spirit Run with this in mind, our connection to the Spirit.

Benny Fillmore (left) and John Snooks (Washo) plyaing hand game. Photo by Laura Fillmore, 1995.

Today's Games

Indian football, hoop and pole, hand game, dice—with a few exceptions, all the California tribes had their own versions of these major games, adapting them to their own ways of life. Footballs made of stone or stuffed deerhide, ring-and-pin games of fishbones or pumpkin rinds, dolls of kelp or clay all reflect the landscapes of their origin and the resourcefulness of their makers.

Anthropologists are fascinated with the cultural and linguistic landscape of native California, where, at one time, there were as many as six hundred autonomous tribal groups. (In fact, the huge number of these groups and their small size continue to generate much discussion of what constitutes a "tribe" in California.) In many parts of the state, few people ever traveled more than twenty miles from the places where they were born, and trade—pine nuts for abalone, obsidian for dentalia, salt for animal skins—was the major opportunity for interaction between tribes. Games traveled along with goods. We can imagine, for example, a Wailaki trader long ago thinking his children might like a ring-and-pin game like the ones that Yurok people made from salmon vertebrae. If the game caught on, the demand would soon surpass the local supply of salmon bones, and the Wailaki ring-and-pin game, as it became established, might be made from deer bones instead. Or another group might have copied the game, but with only eight bones on the cord instead of ten, because that was more in harmony with their own counting system or ritual numbers.

By 1769, when Spanish missionaries arrived, native Californians had been copying and adapting bits and pieces of each others' cultures for centuries. Determined to build an agricultural empire to support their plans for the "new world," the missionaries now recruited Indian people from San Diego to Sonoma, for their souls and for their labor. In the face of disease, exhaustion, malnutrition, and virtual enslavement, native people continued to entertain themselves in the old ways when they could. Without doubt, regional variations of games and toys blurred and shifted throughout

Washo women gambling with European-style playing cards in Reno, Nevada (no date). Photo courtesy of The Huntington Library, San Marino, California, No. 275-05(03).

this period, and it was at this time that native Californians began to add European games to their repertoire. Monte, for instance, was one of the first European card games in California and the Southwest. In the Southwest, Apache players made decks of cards from animal hides and rubbed red, yellow, black, and blue dyes into them. The court cards, simple figures with decorated shields, have the dynamic quality of rock art. Though California Indians didn't manufacture decks of cards, this game fit easily into their gambling traditions, and European-style decks have joined stick dice, shell dice, and bones in the array of traditional gambling implements.

By the time the California Gold Rush was over, Europeans had come to dominate the entire state, and the native population had been nearly destroyed: by introduced diseases to which they had no immunity; by land-hungry settlers and soldiers who treated them as if they were less than human; by the loss of their homes and sustenance; and by the grief that necessarily follows such disasters. From the late 19th century on, anthropologists studied California cultures in great numbers and with great intensity, believing they would soon disappear. A few scholars noted that some of the children's games they came across could have been introduced by Europeans—a Choinumni game of jacks, for instance, or a game that resembled "London Bridge"—but much of what they recorded was derived entirely from native traditions.

Next, the government of the United States took a series of actions designed to channel Native Americans into mainstream American culture. Forced to attend boarding schools away from their homes and families, and punished for speaking their languages, many children gave up the old ways. To ensure that their own children would not have to endure such traumas, some decided never to teach them the languages or customs of their people. Some children ran away from the boarding schools, and a few who stayed clung stubbornly to what they could remember of tribal ways. People who attended the schools recall hiding from school officials to sing and dance and speak their languages and tell the old stories.

At boarding schools, Indian children learned trades that were supposed to ease their adoption of the American way of life. They also learned baseball, basketball, and other European games, and learned them well. On reservations and elsewhere, government agents and missionaries encouraged Indian people to abandon the old gambling games and take up new sports, such as rodeo riding. California was blessed with an abundance of Indian cowboys, and everyone, native and non-native alike, made bets on the side.

Describing a first fruits festival (a traditional spring celebration) in San Diego County in 1934, a journalist wrote, "On the second day the religious ceremonies were

Hupa girls playing basketball (no date). Photo courtesy of The Huntington Library, San Marino, California, No. 056 A-16-4.

Top: Stunts on horseback at the Morongo Reservation near Banning, about 1919. Photo courtesy of The Huntington Library, San Marino, California, No. 039(114). Bottom: Garcia River (Pomo) baseball players. Photo courtesy of the Hearst Museum of Anthropology, No. 15-2702.

repeated and then came another barbecue. Then followed the games of *peon, pelota, gome,* and *monte*—played by the older men, for the younger ones have taken to baseball." If anyone ever wondered where the energy that used to go into playing shinny, hoop and pole, and other native California field games went, much of the answer would have to be baseball. There are teams and regularly scheduled games in virtually every Indian community in the state, and a healthy share of pro players have come from California. John Tortes Meyers, for instance, was from Cahuilla country in southern California. Chief Meyers, as he was called in baseball, was born in 1880. He began playing professional baseball after several years at Dartmouth, joining the New York Giants in 1908. He was the regular catcher for the Giants from 1910 to 1916, and according to sportswriter Lawrence Ritter, he was "widely recognized, by teammates and opponents alike, as the best all-around catcher in the major leagues… and also far and away the hardest-hitting catcher in the game." Besides Meyers, there have been at least two other Cahuilla players in professional baseball—Leroy Alvarez and Mickey Mallory. And today, Matt LaChapa of the Mesa Grande Reservation (Kumeyaay) is, in one of those ironic twists of fate, playing on the San Diego Padres' minor league team.

Baseball, track, football, hockey, basketball, wrestling: these sports all have their parallels in native games, and it may be that extraordinary Indian athletes today reflect a tradition that has defeated all attempts to conquer it: a tradition in which cultivating skill and grace is not considered vain or frivolous, but is instead understood to be one of the things humans must do to make their way in this physical world.

But what about the old games, the way it was before? There is a movement afoot to reintroduce the games where they have been forgotten or neglected. This is part of a much larger movement to revive traditional cultures and find ways for them to work in the modern world.

A man from the Colorado River area describes the excruciatingly slow place at which his people are bringing their language back into common use. Eloquently, he describes the ways in which recovering the language will keep old values from disappearing. Meanwhile, a Las Vegas-style tribal casino has sprung up—overnight, it seems—in the desert. The builders cleared away a huge expanse of mesquite, a plant as important to the desert tribes as oak trees are in the rest of California, without thinking twice.

Elsewhere, a young woman reminisces about the last day she spent with her grandmother, who was the last fluent speaker of their language. They would spend time together doing ordinary things, but speaking in their language as much as possible. They visited the tribe's new casino on that last day. Her grandmother was proud of the impressive building, and even won a little money. It takes ingenuity to use a language that has had no chance to adapt to the changes of the past hundred years, but people manage, often coining new words based on old customs.

At a workshop for California Indians about gathering oral histories, a roomful of people listens raptly to an explanation of the intricacies of video equipment. "I used to have this misconception that Indian people were victims, downtrodden," says the speaker. "But I've learned that they fought all the way… The only thing is, all the old people say they [whites] were like gremlins—you'd get rid of one and hundreds more would show up. This is the history we need to know, this is why it is so important to have native historians and recorders."

A woman whose people long ago lost the last speakers of their language, the singers and dancers and doctors, buys a microfilm reader so she can have the luxury of studying linguistic and ethnographic archives in her own home. A woman from an "extinct" tribe carves a soapstone bowl. It is the most recent in a vast collection of such bowls made by her people, and it is the first in two hundred years. In northwestern California, native women and the Forest Service are finally working together to ensure that plants traditionally used for basketry will be plentiful and suitable to work with. Throughout California, Indian people are blending old and new technologies, finding pride in a heritage that has somehow survived attempts to conquer it by force, assimilation, and misrepresentation.

On a chilly but sunny San Francisco morning, a festival of traditional California Indian games opens with Pomo singing and dancing. The music is dwarfed by the sounds of the city. On one section of a vast lawn, a woman shows children how to play stick dice. Some girls learn the game and are soon teaching it to others. A boy watches curiously, but decides not to get in the game because he's heard that for his people, stick dice is a women's game. Someone tries to get a game of Indian football started, but few people there have ever played, and they don't know each other. The game is stilted and fades out as players drift away. By a formal, arty-looking fountain, people stop to watch a young man as his graceful hands create a complex string figure. "Where did you learn that?" asks his girlfriend, visibly impressed, as they stroll away.

At another gathering, park rangers patiently roll hoops for children to throw poles at. None of the children has ever tried this game before, and it looks like the rangers will have to roll a lot of hoops before anyone makes a point. A bearish-looking boy of about eleven watches for a while, then hefts a pole and succeeds in piercing the hoop on his second try. "I told you I could do it," he says to his little brother. At a southern California fiesta, young men in motorcycle regalia pick up gourd rattles and peon pieces, easily joining the subtle camaraderie of the older men. At a hand-game tournament, players encourage a woman—a relative who has been away from tribal life for a long time—to join the game. Quietly, subtly, they watch out for her, jogging her memory from time to time and making sure she feels she is a part of the team.

Tentatively at times, boldly at others, with successes and failures, California Indian people are trying to restore continuity to their disrupted ways of life. From the memories of those stubborn children who would not give in to the boarding school teachers, from the notes and recordings of anthropologists, from family stories, and sometimes from elders who have managed to live, uninterrupted, a traditional life, California Indians are regaining their heritage: languages, songs, stories, and ceremonies, a traditional sense of family, propriety, wealth, spirituality, and nature. The process brings joys, challenges, and the hope of a way of life made whole. The games, too, are part of it.

LINGUISTIC SYMBOLS

There is no standard orthography for California's many native languages. Usually, vowels are pronounced approximately as they are in Spanish:

a as in father
e as in hello
i as in Tina
o as in over
u as in hula

At one time it was the norm to divide words into syllables with hyphens ("saw'-kahn," "poo-lee chee-nah," etc.). This was meant to simplify pronunciation for the reader, and has no effect on the accompanying sounds. An acute accent (´) indicates that the syllable in which it appears is stressed more than the others. Some other symbols that appear in this book:

> ' or ʔ   *(ku'ig, Kawiiʔa)*. These symbols indicate a glottal stop—a distinct break between syllables, as in "uh-oh."
>
> ɨ   *(pɨ)*. This is a lax vowel, like the "a" in "sofa."
>
> š   *(alkuš-moltmil)*. Pronounced like the "sh" in "ship."

A double vowel, e.g. "oo" usually indicates that the sound is drawn out—pronounced longer than a single vowel. This sound is also sometimes indicated by placing a colon (:) or a raised dot (·) after a vowel. Some scholars, however, have spelled out words with English vowel sounds in mind. Frank Latta's work with the Yokuts languages is an example of this. Thus, the "oo" sound in "Coo'-choon," the villain in Henry Lawrence's Yowlumni Yokuts story, is pronounced as in "soon."

BIBLIOGRAPHY

Baca, Lorenzo. 1986. *Songs, Dances, and Traditions of the Tuolumne Band of California Miwoks.* Dissertation.

Barrett, S.A. 1919. *Myths of the Southern Sierra Miwok.* University of California Publications in American Archaeology and Ethnology, Vol. 16, No. 1. Berkeley: University of California Press.

Beals, Ralph L. 1933. *Ethnology of the Nisenan.* University of California Publications in American Archaeology and Anthropology, Vol. 31, No. 6. Berkeley: University of California Press.

Bibby, Brian. 1994. "Field Games of Native California." In *News from Native California* 8(1):18-22.

Blackburn, Thomas C. 1975. *December's Child: A Book of Chumash Oral Narratives.* Berkeley: University of California Press.

Cuero, Delfina: *see* Shipek, Florence

Culin, Stewart. 1992. *Games of the North American Indians* (Vols. 1 & 2). Lincoln & London: University of Nebraska Press. Orig. printed as *Games of the North American Indians,* Twenty-Fourth Annual Report of the Bureau of American Ethnology, 1902–1903, Smithsonian Institution (1907).

Curl, Jenny: *see* DuBois, Cora & Dorothy Demetracopoulou.

Dixon, Roland. 1907. *The Shasta.* Bulletin of the American Museum of Natural History, Vol. 17, Article 5. New York: American Museum of Natural History.

Downs, James F. 1961. *Washo Religion.* Anthropological Records, Vol. 16, No. 9. Berkeley: University of California Press.

Driver, Harold Edson. 1936. *Wappo Ethnography.* University of California Publications in American Archaeology and Ethnology, Vol. 36, No. 3. Berkeley: University of California Press.

Drucker, Philip. 1937. *The Tolowa and their Southwest Oregon Kin.* University of California Publications in American Archaeology and Ethnology, Vol. 36, No. 4. Berkeley: University of California Press.

DuBois, Constance Goddard. 1908. *The Religion of the Luiseño Indians of Southern California.* University of California Publications in American Archaeology and Ethnology, Vol. 8, No. 3. Berkeley: University of California Press.

DuBois, Cora. 1935. *Wintu Ethnography.* University of California Publications in American Archaeology and Ethnology, Vol. 36, No. 1. Berkeley: University of California Press.

Du Bois, Cora and Dorothy Demetracopoulou. 1931. *Wintu Myths.* University of California Publications in American Archaeology and Ethnology, Vol. 28, No. 5. Berkeley: University of California Press.

Forde, Cyril Daryll. 1931. *Ethnography of the Yuma Indians.* University of California Publications in American Archaeology and Ethnology, Vol. 28, No. 4. Berkeley: University of California Press.

Foster, George. 1944. *A Summary of Yuki Culture.* Anthropological Records, Vol. 5, No. 3. Berkeley: University of California Press.

Garbani, Ledonna. 1993. *Handgames: A Native American Indian Family Tradition.* Placerville: Ledonna Garbani.

Garth, Thomas Russell. 1953. *Atsugewi Ethnography.* Anthropological Records, Vol. 14, No. 2. Berkeley: University of California Press.

Gayton, A. H. (Anna Hadwick). 1940. *Yokuts and Western Mono Myths.* Anthropological Records Vol. 5, No. 1. Berkeley: University of California Press.

Gifford, Edward Winslow. 1917. *Miwok Myths.* University of California Publications in American Archaeology and Ethnology, Vol. 12, No. 8. Berkeley: University of California Press.

Goddard, Pliny. 1903. *Life and Culture of the Hupa.* University of California Publications in American Archaeology and Anthropology, Vol. 1, No. 1. Berkeley: University of California Press.

Goldschmidt, Walter R. 1951. *Nomlaki Ethnography.* University of California Publications in American Archaeology and Ethnology, Vol. 42, No. 4. Berkeley: University of California Press.

Heizer, Robert F. 1968. *The Indians of Los Angeles County: Hugo Reid's Letters of 1852.* Southwest Museum Papers No. 21. Los Angeles: Southwest Museum.

Hinton, Leanne. 1994. *Flutes of Fire: Essays on California Indian Languages.* Berkeley: Heyday Books.

Holt, Catherine. 1946. *Shasta Ethnography.* Anthropological Records, Vol. 3, No. 4. Berkeley: University of California Press.

Hooper, Lucile. 1920. *The Cahuilla Indians.* University of California Publications in American Archaeology and Ethnology, Vol. 16, No. 6. Berkeley: University of California Press.

Jayne, Caroline Furness. 1962. *String Figures and How to Make Them: A Study of Cats-Cradle in Many Lands.* New York: Dover Books. Orig. printed as *String Figures,* Charles Scribner's Sons (1906).

Jones, Jeff. *see* Goldschmidt, Walter R.

Joseph, William. *see* Uldall, Hans

Kelly, Isabel T. 1932. *Ethnography of the Surprise Valley Paiute.* University of California Publications in American Archaeology and Ethnology, Vol. 31, No. 3. Berkeley: University of California Press.

Klasky, Philip. 1992. "Spirit Run." In *News from Native California* 6(4):19-20.

Kroeber, A.L. 1907. *Indian Myths of South Central California.* University of California Publications in American Archaeology and Ethnology, Vol. 4, No. 4. Berkeley: University of California Press.

—1948. *Seven Mohave Myths.* Anthropological Records, Vol. 11, No. 1. Berkeley: University of California Press.

—1976. *Handbook of the Indians of California.* New York: Dover Publications. Orig. printed as Bureau of American Ethnology, Bulletin 78, Government Printing Office (1925).

Laird, Carobeth. 1976. *The Chemehuevis.* Banning: Malki Museum Press.

Latta, Frank F. 1977 *Handbook of Yokuts Indians.* Santa Cruz: Bear State Books.

—n.d. unpublished notes at Yosemite National Park Research Library.

Lawrence, Henry. *see* Latta, Frank

Librado, Fernando. 1977. *The Eye of the Flute: Chumash Traditional History and Ritual* as told to John P. Harrington. Santa Barbara Bicentennial Historical Series, No. 4. Santa Barbara: Santa Barbara Museum of Natural History.

Loeb, Edwin. 1926. *Pomo Folkways.* University of California Publications in American Archaeology and Ethnology, Vol. 19, No. 2. Berkeley: University of California Press.

—1989. *The Western Kuksu Cult.* University of California Publications in American Archaeology and Ethnology, Vol. 33, No. 1. Berkeley: University of California Press.

Lowie, Robert H. 1939. *Ethnographic Notes on the Washo.* University of California Publications in American Archaeology and Ethnology, Vol. 36, No. 5. Berkeley: University of California Press.

Lucas, Bun (as told to Bev Ortiz). "Playing Leaves." In *News from Native California* 8(1):45.

Mayfield, Thomas Jefferson. 1994. *Indian Summer.* Berkeley: Heyday Books.

McNichols, Charles. 1967. *Crazy Weather.* Lincoln: University of Nebraska Press, Bison Books.

Miranda, Mike. *see* Voegelin, Charles

Nabokov, Peter. 1987. *Indian Running.* Santa Fe: Ancient City Press.

Nomland, Gladys Ayer. 1938. *Bear River Ethnography.* Anthropological Records, Vol. 2, No. 2. Berkeley: University of California Press.

Ortiz, Bev. 1994. "Kashaya Kelp Dolls." In *News from Native California*, 8(1):43
—1992. "Patient Tasks." In *News from Native California* 6(4):14-18.

Oswalt, Robert. 1964 *Kashaya Texts.* University of California Publications in Linguistics, Vol. 36. Berkeley: University of California Press.

Parker, Lucy. 1994. "Miwok Games." In *News from Native California* 8(1):28-29.

Parrish, Essie. *see* Oswalt, Robert

Patterson, Victoria. 1994. "Playing for Real." In *News from Native California* 8(1):30-33.

Peri, David. 1987. "The Game of Staves." In *News from Native California* 1(3):5-7.

Potts, Marie. 1991. *The Northern Maidu.* Happy Camp: Naturegraph Publishers.

Reid, Hugo. *see* Heizer, Robert

Ritter, Lawrence. 1985. *The Glory of Their Times: The Story of the Early Days of Baseball Told by the Men who Played it.* New York: Vintage Books.

Sapir, Edward and Leslie Spier. 1943. *Notes on the Culture of the Yana.* Anthropological Records, Vol. 3, No. 3. Berkeley: University of California Press.

Schoenherr, Allan A. 1992. *A Natural History of California.* Berkeley, Los Angeles and Oxford: University of California Press.

Shipek, Florence Connolly. 1991. *Delfina Cuero: Her Autobiography, an Account of Her Last Years, and her Ethnobotanic Contributions.* Menlo Park: Ballena Press.

Sparkman, Philip Stedman. 1908. *Culture of the Luiseño Indians.* University of California Publications in American Archaeology and Ethnology, Vol. 8, No. 4. Berkeley: University of California Press.

Spier, Leslie. 1923. *Southern Diegueño Customs.* University of California Publications in American Archaeology and Ethnology, Vol. 20, No. 16. Berkeley: University of California Press.

Steward, Julian H. 1936. *Myths of the Owens Valley Paiute.* University of California Publications in American Archaeology and Ethnology, Vol. 34, No. 5. Berkeley: University of California Press.

——1933. *Ethnography of Owens Valley Paiute.* University of California Publications in American Archaeology and Ethnology, Vol. 33, No. 3. Berkeley: University of California Press.

Strike, Sandra S. 1994. *Ethnobotany of the California Indians.* Vol. 2; Illinois: Koeltz Scientific Books.

Tac, Pablo. 1952. *Indian Life and Customs at Mission San Luis Rey: A Record of California Mission Life by Pablo Tac, an Indian Neophyte; written at Rome about 1835.* Edited and translated with an historical introduction by Minna and Gordon Hewes. Reprinted from *The Americas.*

Thompson, Lucy (Che-na-wah Weitch-ah-wah). 1991. *To the American Indian: Reminiscences of a Yurok Woman,* Berkeley: Heyday Books.

Uldall, Hans and William Shipley. 1966. *Nisenan Texts and Dictionary.* University of California Publications in Linguistics, Vol. 46. Berkeley: University of California Press.

Voegelin, Charles. 1935. *Tubatulabal Texts.* University of California Publications in American Archaeology and Ethnology, Vol. 34, No. 3. Berkeley: University of California Press.

Voegelin, Erminie Wheeler. 1938. *Tubatulabal Ethnography.* Anthropological Records, Vol. 2, No. 1. Berkeley: University of California Press.

Webb, Edith Buckland. 1952. *Indian Life at the Old Missions.* Los Angeles: Warren F. Lewis.

Yamane, Linda. 1994. "Bringing the Games Back Home." In *News from Native California* 8(1):34-35.

INDEX

Also Published by Heyday Books

News from Native California
An Inside View of the Indian World

A quarterly magazine written and produced by California Indians and those close to the Indian community, *News from Native California* provides an intimate portrait of traditional and contemporary California Indian culture and history. Each issue has lively columns and features on art, language, literature, political concerns, traditional skills, and ongoing and upcoming events, and is illustrated with dozens of historical and contemporary photos.
Single copies: $4.95/one year subscriptions: $19.00

Native American Titles

The Way We Lived: California Indian Stories, Songs and Reminiscences
Edited with commentary by Malcolm Margolin, $14.95

The Ohlone Way: Indian Life in the San Francisco–Monterey Bay Area
Malcolm Margolin, $14.95

The Maidu Indian Myths and Stories of Hanc'ibyjim
Edited and translated by William Shipley, $12.95

Indian Summer: Traditional Life among the Choinumne Indians of California's San Joaquin Valley
Thomas Jefferson Mayfield, $13.95

To the American Indian: Reminiscences of a Yurok Woman
Lucy Thompson (Che-na-wah Weitch-ah-wah), $14.95

Flutes of Fire: Essays on California Indian Languages
Leanne Hinton, $18.00

How to Keep Your Language Alive: A Commonsense Approach to One-on-One Language Learning
Leanne Hinton, $15.95

Dream Songs and Ceremony: Reflections on Traditional California Indian Dance
Frank LaPena, $25.00

Straight with the Medicine: Narratives of Washoe Followers of the Tipi Way
Warren L. d'Azevedo, $12.95

It Will Live Forever: Traditional Yosemite Indian Acorn Preparation
Beverly R. Ortiz, as told by Julia Parker, $13.95

Children's Books

Native Ways: California Indian Stories and Memories
Edited by Malcolm Margolin and Yolanda Montijo, $10.95

Adopted by Indians: A True Story
Thomas Jefferson Mayfield, $ 10.95

Lion Singer
Sylvia Ross, $12.95

For information on ordering our books or subscribing to News from Native California, *please contact us at:*

Heyday Books
P.O. Box 9145
Berkeley, CA 94709
(510) 549-3564 (510) 549-1889 fax
www.heydaybooks.com

HEYDAY INSTITUTE

Since its founding in 1974, Heyday Books has occupied a unique niche in the publishing world, specializing in books that foster an understanding of the history, literature, art, environment, social issues, and culture of California and the West. We are a 501(c)(3) nonprofit organization based in Berkeley, California, serving a wide range of people and audiences.

We are grateful for the generous funding we've received for our publications and programs during the past year from foundations and more than 300 individual donors. Major supporters include:

Anonymous; Anthony Andreas, Jr., Barnes & Noble bookstores; Bay Tree Fund; S.D. Bechtel, Jr. Foundation; California Council for the Humanities; California Oak Foundation; Candelaria Fund; Columbia Foundation; Colusa Indian Community Council; Federated Indians of Graton Rancheria; Wallace Alexander Gerbode Foundation; Richard & Rhoda Goldman Fund; Evelyn & Walter Haas, Jr. Fund; Walter & Elise Haas Fund; Hopland Band of Pomo Indians; James Irvine Foundation; George Frederick Jewett Foundation; LEF Foundation; David Mas Masumoto; Michael McCone; Middletown Rancheria Tribal Council; Gordon & Betty Moore Foundation; Morongo Band of Mission Indians; National Endowment for the Arts; National Park Service; Poets & Writers; Rim of the World Interpretive Association; River Rock Casino; Alan Rosenus; San Francisco Foundation; John-Austin Saviano/Moore Foundation; Sandy Cold Shapero; Ernest & June Siva; L.J. Skaggs and Mary C. Skaggs Foundation; Swinerton Family Fund; Victorian Alliance; Susan Swig Watkins; and the Harold & Alma White Memorial Fund.

For more information about Heyday Institute, our publications and programs, please visit our website at www.heydaybooks.com.

About the Author

Jeannine Gendar is an editor and writer and has been working with California Indian communities since 1987. She was managing editor of *News from Native California*, a quarterly magazine devoted to California Indian history and ongoing culture, from 1990 to 2000. She is trying to grow enough milkweed for string figures in her native plant gardens in Martinez, California.